THE FACE OF

San Francisco

The Face of

SAN FRANCISCO

Text by HAROLD GILLIAM

Photographs by PHIL PALMER

DOUBLEDAY & COMPANY, INC., *Garden City, N.Y., 1960*

Library of Congress Catalog Card Number 60–15174

Copyright © 1960 by Harold Thompson Gilliam and Philip S. Palmer

All Rights Reserved

Printed in the United States of America

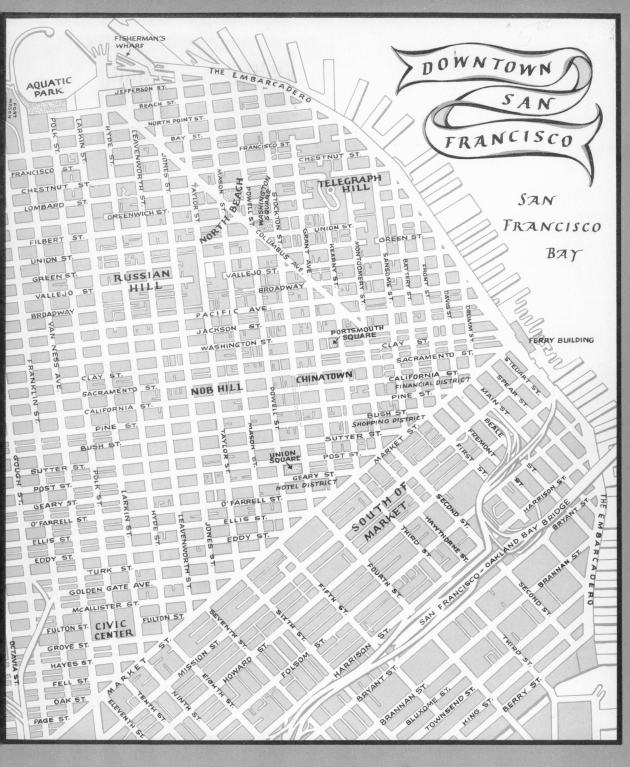

DOWNTOWN SAN FRANCISCO

SAN FRANCISCO BAY

FISHERMAN'S WHARF

AQUATIC PARK

THE EMBARCADERO

JEFFERSON ST.
BEACH ST.
NORTH POINT ST.
BAY ST.
FRANCISCO ST.
CHESTNUT ST.
FRANCISCO ST.
CHESTNUT ST.
LOMBARD ST.
GREENWICH ST.
FILBERT ST.
UNION ST.
GREEN ST.
VALLEJO ST.
BROADWAY
PACIFIC AVE.
JACKSON ST.
WASHINGTON ST.

TELEGRAPH HILL

NORTH BEACH

RUSSIAN HILL

UNION ST.
GREEN ST.

VALLEJO ST.
BROADWAY

PORTSMOUTH SQUARE

CHINATOWN

NOB HILL

CLAY ST.
SACRAMENTO ST.
CALIFORNIA ST.
PINE ST.
BUSH ST.

CALIFORNIA ST.
FINANCIAL DISTRICT
PINE ST.
BUSH ST.
SHOPPING DISTRICT
SUTTER ST.

FERRY BUILDING

CLAY ST.
SACRAMENTO ST.

UNION SQUARE

POST ST.

GEARY ST.
HOTEL DISTRICT

SUTTER ST.
POST ST.
GEARY ST.
O'FARRELL ST.
ELLIS ST.
EDDY ST.

O'FARRELL ST.
ELLIS ST.
EDDY ST.

TURK ST.
GOLDEN GATE AVE.
MCALLISTER ST.

FULTON ST.
FULTON ST.

CIVIC CENTER

GROVE ST.
HAYES ST.
FELL ST.
OAK ST.
PAGE ST.

SOUTH OF MARKET

MARKET ST.

SAN FRANCISCO – OAKLAND BAY BRIDGE

THE EMBARCADERO

MISSION ST.
HOWARD ST.
FOLSOM ST.
HARRISON ST.
BRYANT ST.
BRANNAN ST.
TOWNSEND ST.
KING ST.
BERRY ST.

FORT MASON
POLK ST.
LARKIN ST.
HYDE ST.
LEAVENWORTH ST.
JONES ST.
TAYLOR ST.
MASON ST.
POWELL ST.
WASHINGTON ST.
STOCKTON ST.
COLUMBUS AVE.
GRANT AVE.
KEARNY ST.
MONTGOMERY ST.
SANSOME ST.
BATTERY ST.
FRONT ST.
DAVIS ST.
DRUMM ST.
STEUART ST.
SPEAR ST.
MAIN ST.
BEALE ST.
FREMONT ST.
FIRST ST.
SECOND ST.
HAWTHORNE ST.
THIRD ST.
FOURTH ST.
FIFTH ST.
SIXTH ST.
SEVENTH ST.
EIGHTH ST.
NINTH ST.
TENTH ST.
ELEVENTH ST.
HARRISON ST.
BRYANT ST.
SECOND ST.
THIRD ST.
BRANNAN ST.
BLUXOME ST.

GOUGH ST.
FRANKLIN AVE.
VAN NESS AVE.
POLK ST.
LARKIN ST.
HYDE ST.
LEAVENWORTH ST.
JONES ST.
TAYLOR ST.
MASON ST.
OCTAVIA ST.
MARKET ST.

San Francisco

map by palacios

Contents

"Harbor Queen"

Oakland, Broadway

ACKNOWLEDGMENTS

The writer could not have produced his part of this book without the generous help and advice of experts in various fields—none of whom is to be held responsible for any of the writer's statements of fact or opinion. Special thanks are due to James W. Keilty, senior city planner of the San Francisco Department of City Planning, whose intimate knowledge of contemporary San Francisco was of inestimable help in the preparation of several sections of the manuscript. Among others whose assistance was invaluable were William Wilson Wurster, dean of the College of Architecture at the University of California in Berkeley; Clifford E. Paine, builder of the Golden Gate Bridge; Edward Howden, chief of the California Fair Employment Practices Division; Earl Raab, associate director of the Jewish Community Relations Council; Rev. Hamilton Boswell, pastor of the Jones Methodist Church; Henry S. Tom, executive secretary of the Chinese Branch of the Y.M.C.A.; Rose Chew, staff consultant of the International Institute; H. K. Wong, publicity director of the Chinese Chamber of Commerce; Carmelo Zito, publisher of *Il Corriere del Popolo;* Masao W. Satow, national director of the Japanese American Citizens League; Alice Slater, director of the Information Bureau, and Roy L. Hudson, supervisor of maintenance, San Francisco Recreation and Park Department; David Nelson, assistant to the director, San Francisco Maritime Museum; Polly Mansfield, expert on present-day San Francisco; John Reber, pioneer in regional planning for the Bay Area; Alfred Frankenstein, music and art critic, Stanleigh Arnold, Sunday editor, and Thelma Weber, librarian—all of the San Francisco *Chronicle.*

Above all, the writer is indebted beyond measure for the continuous assistance and inspiration of Ann Lawrence Gilliam, who collaborated on all sections of this book and, with minor exceptions, wrote Chapter IV in its entirety.

For further reading on some of the subjects discussed in this book the reader is referred to *Golden Gate, Park of a Thousand Vistas,* by Katherine Wilson, *Around the World in San Francisco,* by Leonard Austin (a guide to ethnic groups), and *San Francisco, the Bay and Its Cities,* a W.P.A. guidebook.

For his part of this book the writer would make a double dedication:

To RODNEY GILLIAM, *1893–1959*
and
GREGORY GILLIAM, *1959–*

THE FACE OF
San Francisco

North Beach;
Columbus Avenue

Listen to the wind that blows from the west, lifting banners of spindrift from the crests of waves off the Cliff House, bending the limbs of the oaks in Golden Gate Park, tightening the strings of kites flown by boys on the Marina Green. Listen to the wind, for it brings to the imagination the sounds of the past. . . .

It brings the sounds that were here before the coming of man—the pounding of the waves of the rocky headlands of the Golden Gate, the primeval roar of the sea lions on Seal Rocks, the honking of long flocks of wild geese high over the white sand of Ocean Beach, the chants of oborigines around ancient campfires, the sharp explosions of the muskets of Drake as his crew hunts seals on the Farallones, the first clear note of the bell at Mission Dolores ringing out across the grassy valley by the lagoon.

Listen to the wind that comes over the hills, whipping the waters of the bay into whitecaps, flapping shirts on clotheslines in the Sunset District, knocking off the hats of the tourists on the cable cars at Union Square. Listen to the wind, for you will hear the sounds of history—the roll of drums and the call of the bugle as Lt. Montgomery raises the Stars and Stripes in Portsmouth Plaza, the bellow of Sam Brannan shouting, "Gold!" the trample of feet, the splash of anchors, the sound of ten thousand voices talking bonanza, the sudden bursts of pistol fire, the quick, decisive snap of the Vigilantes' noose. Listen and hear the labored chug of the first locomotive arriving from across the continent, the sharp crackling of canvas on windjammers standing into the Golden Gate, the churning of a hundred paddle wheels on steamboats and ferries plying the bay.

Listen to the wind that blows into spray the geysers of whales spouting off Point Lobos, ripples the grasses and the lupine on the slopes of Twin Peaks, rattles the windows in the houses of Telegraph Hill. Listen and you will hear the sudden thunder of collapsing walls as the earth shudders, the sickening roar of a holocaust, and then the ancient rhythmic sound of the pounding hammer. Listen to the rattle of riveters and the clang of steel during the building of the world's biggest bridges, the crack of gunfire on the docks in the Great Strike, the blare of the bands in the fair at Treasure Island, the wail of the Ferry Building siren as the lights of the city go out after Pearl Harbor, the rap of the gavel on the podium of the Opera House at the founding of the United Nations.

Listen to the wind, for the past is prelude, and the sounds rising from the city this moment will become the sounds of history.

Russian Hill; Taylor Street

Oakland from Berkeley

Washington Street

From Vista Point, Marin County

CHAPTER I

City of Paradox

Define the city at your peril.

Call it sophisticated and cosmopolitan—which it is—and you find it smug and provincial—which it also is. Call it beautiful and you discover blatant ugliness. Call it ugly and you are confronted with surpassing beauty.

With infinite elusiveness San Francisco escapes definition, evades all attempts to pin it down, contradicts whatever generalizations you may make about it.

See it from the Bay Bridge early in the day, when the ships are moving into the docks at its base; the morning light blazes from its windows; the flags on its towers fly like banners in the cool salt breeze from the Golden Gate. The skyscrapers on its hills seem almost geologic—as if some sudden upheaval of earth had raised this peninsula and then, bursting the limitations of rock, had thrust into the sky these towers of light.

At such a moment it seems to be a city in a vision. It is a symbol of the perennial human dream—the legendary City of Man, goal of the long westward migrations, rising above the waters here at the ultimate shore of the New World, full of secret promise and unknown fulfillment.

But enter the city and the vision fades; a thousand conflicting impressions crowd the senses—the brilliance of sunlight and the misty dimness of fogs, the fragrance of the sea winds and the acrid smells of industry, the clamor of the commercial districts and the quiet serenity of the hilltops. You look up from the frenetic traffic of the downtown streets to the soaring towers of a bridge across the sky. You look out from a dark, cluttered alley to the brilliant aquamarine expanse of the great bay shining in the sun. You are possessed by the continual anticipation that some new revelation is always just around the corner or over the next hill, tantalizing and unnamable.

Go into the city and climb its heights, explore its hidden lanes and cellar cafés, roam the green avenues of its parks, watch the floods of fog pour over the hills and through the streets, listen to the solemn chorus of great horns from the bay. Study its buildings: the skyscrapers of the financial district, the saloons and flophouses of skid row, the intricately scrolled Victorian houses, the long rows of bay-windowed flats undulating over the hills, the white mansions of Pacific Heights, the red brick pagoda-roofed buildings of Chinatown. Talk with its people: its bankers and longshoremen and socialites and cable-car conductors, its residents whose ancestors came from the banks of the Arno, the Seine, the Congo, the Si-kiang.

Go into the city and seek its identity, and you will find only contradictions and conflicts that defy attempts to fit them into a consistent pattern of meaning.

You will find a city that cultivates to a high degree the fine arts and the graces of living—and a city that is exceeded by few others in its appalling rates of alcoholism and suicide. Its art museums, its symphony orchestra, its opera company are among the finest in the nation; its library, its city hospital, its home for the aged are perennially inadequate and recurrently in need of financial transfusions.

It venerates such symbols of the past as its cable-car lines but persistently curtails them. It is proud of its classic Civic Center but fails to expand it as the city grows. It cherishes its historic buildings but allows them to be demolished one by one.

It maintains racially segregated neighborhoods, but its people are usually willing to accept a man as friend without regard to his color or his religion. It looks back with nostalgia on its historic bohemians but disapproves of its contemporary bohemians. Its greatest tourist attraction is a near slum; its greatest park is a superlative example of creative ingenuity.

It is an old city, bemused by contemplation of its own history, looking forever backward to its legendary Golden Age. It is a young city, born little more than a century ago. With its superb natural harbor, its tall buildings rising in terraces on its hills, its great swinging bridges, its imperial position above the bay and ocean, it is a symbol of youth and vigor and aspiration. Facing across the Pacific the awakening lands of Asia, it confronts a future of illimitable promise.

Simultaneously old and young, decadent and creative, prejudiced and tolerant, ugly and beautiful, it is a city of eternal paradox, baffling comprehension with its irreconcilable conflicts and its infinite diversity. No one has been able finally to name the essence of this city. Every person must seek its identity for himself, must look for its manifold meaning wherever they may be found—along its skyline, on its hills and in its neighborhoods, among its diverse peoples, in its centers of commerce and culture, through its parks, along its beaches, down its boulevards, and in its thousand byways.

For in truth this is the City of Man at the western edge of the world, always on the horizon, never quite attained.

Powell Street, evening

Nob Hill from the west

Russian Hill

Coffee Gallery jam session

Market and New Montgomery Streets

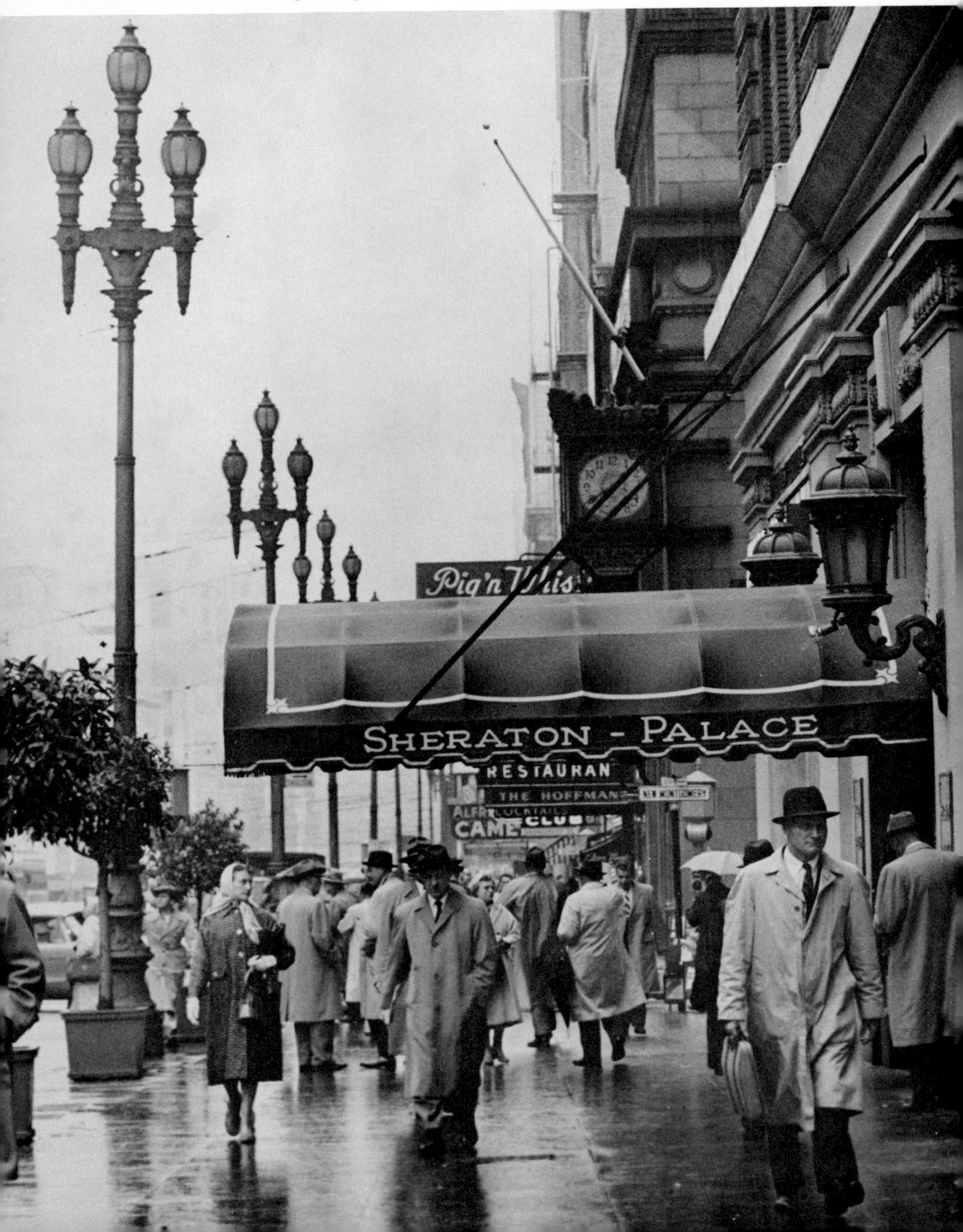

Nob Hill from the north

CHAPTER II

The Skyline

See the skyline of the city from any point of the compass—from a Marin hillside or from the eastern shore of the bay or from the Bayshore Freeway at the point where, coming north, you round a hill and suddenly your vision is assaulted by the combined upthrust of peninsular hills and monoliths of steel.

Let your eye move along the jagged urban profile from the cluster of skyscrapers in the financial district up to the hotels climbing Nob Hill, across to the tall slim apartment houses on Russian Hill, to cylindrical Coit Tower on Telegraph Hill over the Embarcadero, and finally to the great bridges sweeping rhythmically across the dramatic expanse of water to the cities and mountains of the far shore.

Here is surely one of the half-dozen panoramas on the North American Continent with the greatest capacity to excite awe and wonder. Among such sights this skyline is unique; it belongs to neither the world of nature nor the world of man but to both. Here the works of man do not obliterate the natural landscape but rather express and extend it.

Compared to the skyscrapers of New York or Chicago, those of San Francisco are not extraordinarily high. Measured from street level, the tallest structures here are less than half the height of the Empire State Building. But these buildings rise on the hills above the bay in a series of natural terraces, giving the skyline a proportioned spaciousness contrasting sharply with the tightly massed skyscrapers of Manhattan. Not only do the buildings of this city seem to be upward projections of its hills, but they are inseparable from the other elements of the natural scene as well. Wreathed in a white

From the Presidio

mantle of fog or swept clean by the perennial sea winds, the city is bounded by the swiftly flowing tides of the bay, by sharply rising mountains, by long sand beaches and the flat blue expanses of the Pacific.

From a distance, rising steeply up from the water to the hilltops, its flags whipped stiffly eastward by the wind, the city seems indeed, as Bret Harte wrote, "serene, indifferent to fate." But the first impression is deceptive. Imperial and serene as it may seem from a distance, the city is a focus of complex forces that are gradually revealed as you draw nearer and the general view of the skyline dissolves into separate structures.

Observe the city's buildings as you approach and you will see a graphic representation of many of the paradoxes that give San Francisco its fascination. Look carefully and you can see, written in giant symbols across the skyline, a city's search for its own identity.

From the Bayshore freeway

From Vista Point, Marin County

The story of this search can be told in terms of four men who left their distinctive marks on the city's downtown skyline—and of one who did not. All five were architects, and their works illustrate a major contradiction in the city's psyche—the conflict between the eternal human tendency to cling to the traditional and the urge to create new forms expressing new ideas.

An account of the skyline properly begins with one of the city's best-loved symbols—the Ferry Building. For decades thousands of commuters hurried down its echoing corridors twice daily, making it the busiest terminal in the nation, and until the last of the Southern Pacific ferries were suspended in 1958 it was the gateway to the city for all passengers arriving by transcontinental railroad.

It was constructed in the late 1890's, an era when it had not yet occurred to anyone that a new building could be anything but a copy of an older one—preferably one in Europe. Its spire was modeled after Seville's Giralda tower, which itself had been constructed as a Moorish minaret. No muezzin calls the faithful to prayer from the Ferry Building's balcony, but the structure nevertheless has an almost religious significance for San Franciscans. The slim, well-proportioned tower at the foot of Market Street, strikingly illuminated at night, inevitably arouses in old residents nostalgic recollections of the golden days of the commuter ferries and serves as a fitting memorial to that more leisurely era. The old building may well come to serve as a symbol of a new era as well; it is the home of the new World Trade Center, which is concerned with the economic development of the Pacific basin.

When the building's architect, Arthur Page Brown, died in 1896 before construction was well under way, a young assistant named Willis Polk finished the job and thus launched a career that had a lasting effect on the city's skyline. As the leading local architect after the earthquake and fire of 1906, Polk was known as "the man who rebuilt San Francisco." He was a diminutive man of great vanity, greater talent, and an irrepressible propensity for the flamboyant gesture and the devastating remark. In an era of somber clothing for men, he loved to dress in bright colors and flowing capes and often twirled a Malacca cane. He was urged to run for mayor but refused to demean himself with politics. When someone discovered late in his career

erry Building from beneath freeway

that he lacked an architect's license, he retorted that he was no mere architect; he was a "master builder."

Among the fire-gutted buildings he restored after 1906 were the city's first two "skyscrapers," the de Young Building at Kearny and Market and the Claus Spreckels Building (today's Central Tower) on an opposite corner. He later designed and built many new structures; the largest was the Hobart Building, whose curious bulging tower still looms over Market at Second. It was the first Market Street building to be finished architecturally on all four sides so that it appears symmetrical from any angle, in contrast with its neighbors, finished on the street side only. One of the stories often told about Polk took place during the construction of this building when a city inspector appeared to complain that the building's plans did not accord with regulations. Polk at first ignored the official, then, when the latter persisted, hopped on a girder that was about to be hauled upward and was whisked away into the sky.

Although Polk's ability to carry out original ideas was limited—as is that of any architect—by the views of his clients, his final large building gave full scope to his talents and opened a new chapter in the history of American architecture. He was given a free hand by the University of California to design a commercial building for a piece of income property owned by the university on Sutter Street near Montgomery. The structure, completed in 1918, embodied the city's first large-scale architectural innovation—a front "curtain" wall composed of glass, reflecting the sky and nearby buildings on its mirrorlike surface.

The revolutionary structure startled the city. Next to the heavy masonry styles of the period, it appeared flimsy and insubstantial. It was the butt of the inevitable jokes about glass houses, and people went to Sutter Street to stare skeptically as if they expected it to collapse momentarily.

Architects and engineers had known for decades that, with the development of steel-frame buildings, heavy outer walls were no longer necessary; the structures were supported instead by the inner steel skeleton. But out of deference to tradition architects had continued to design buildings with massive or apparently massive walls, even adding false-front columns in the classic Parthenon style. Most of San Francisco's older buildings still have these movie-set façades.

Polk's "glass building" on Sutter Street was proof that architects need no longer cling to the limitations of masonry construction and classic forms but could venture into completely new fields. In this sense Polk's bold innovation was the progenitor of all modern glass and steel construction. Polk himself was not willing to go all the way with glass and felt it necessary to decorate the façade at various intervals with designs of lacy ironwork that contrast curiously with the shining glass wall itself. But even in this use of older forms he showed originality; part of this ironwork consists of the fire escapes, imaginatively woven into the design. Appropriately, Polk's masterpiece was named for another San Francisco innovator—University of California regent Andrew Hallidie, who in 1873 had invented the cable car.

Although the Hallidie Building was so far ahead of its time that it met with a largely negative reception, one San Francisco architect was especially emphatic in its defense. He criticized the decorative ironwork but lauded the building's innovations and had high praise for Polk's "ingenuity and verve." His name was Irving F. Morrow, and he was to be heard from again.

Completely unlike the temperamental Polk was the second of the four architects of the downtown skyline, Arthur Brown, Jr. (He was not related to the Arthur Page Brown who designed the Ferry Building.) Polk had lacked formal schooling and flouted convention at every opportunity, but Brown was a model student at the University of California and did almost everything in the approved manner. There is a story that, as a graduate student at the École des Beaux Arts in Paris, he achieved the highest standing ever attained by an American and proceeded to win so many of the architectural prizes that the school's authorities barred Americans from competing.

Brown's reputation as a prodigy was still new at the time of the 1906 disaster, and when with his partner, John Bakewell, Jr., he won the competition for a design for a new city hall, there was almost unanimous approval. Brown and Bakewell not only lived up to the best Beaux Arts tradition, they considerably exceeded it. The building, completed in 1915, was a triumph of

Hallidie Building

classic proportions, an ornate symbol of civic splendor. The city's mayor, "Sunny Jim" Rolph, beamed with pride at the monumental structure and informed the world on frequent occasions that the building's giant dome was exactly sixteen feet, two and five-eighths inches higher than the U. S. Capitol dome in Washington.

The structure is a judicious combination of Renaissance styles. The interior is as impressive as the classic colonnaded exterior. The great rotunda beneath the dome is not only awe-inspiring in size but is adorned with a lavish wealth of architectural detail. A grand marble staircase flows majestically down from the main gallery. From it the eye moves upward past walls and columns of cut granite, lanterns, arches, vaults, bas-reliefs, statuary groups, bronze and iron ornamentation, and richly balustraded galleries to

City Hall

the mammoth dome itself, high enough to contain a ten-story building. Classic scholar Henry Hope Reed, Jr., writes: "In the just quality of ornament, in the play of space, in the total overwhelming effect, the San Francisco City Hall is the best that American art has produced."

The City Hall was an achievement that Brown could hardly hope to surpass, and it is understandable, in view of his conservative nature, that he proceeded in nearly all of his subsequent buildings, many of them also in partnership with Bakewell, to design variations on the same theme, though necessarily none was as lavishly opulent. The unmistakable marks of his style—glistening cut granite, large gilt lanterns, gracefully columned classic façades, and sculptured heads and figures—are readily identifiable not only in many of the buildings of the Civic Center but even in the Pacific Gas and Electric Company Building on Market Street, built in 1925, his only large commercial structure. The building is particularly striking at night, brilliantly flooded with white light.

The greatest achievement of Brown's later years was the War Memorial Opera House (1932), birthplace of the United Nations. Even Brown the traditionalist recognized that San Francisco should not merely copy the prototype of an opera house set by Milan and Paris and followed by New York in the old Metropolitan. But it was characteristic that in departing from one precedent Brown was following another—at least in part. His model was the work of a man who might be regarded as something of an authority on opera—Richard Wagner.

In designing his opera house at Bayreuth, Wagner, who detested the fashion-show aspects of opera, was concerned with emphasizing the performance and de-emphasizing the audience. His music-dramas demanded a structure carrying out the modern concept of a theater. Instead of allowing most of the spectators to stare at each other from opposite wings of a giant horseshoe, he sternly faced the seats to the front. He omitted the grand staircase and foyer, which in traditional opera houses had been used primarily for the parades of the aristocracy, lowered the orchestra and conductor out of sight, and expanded the stage.

Brown's design combined some of the Wagnerian reforms with certain concessions to tradition such as the single row of boxes along the side walls.

Opera House

Embellished in his own classic style, the result was a structure of compelling beauty. Brown also designed the opera's twin edifice, the Veterans Building next door.

If Wagner was the greatest influence on Brown in the design of the Opera House, it may be that a woman was the most important influence on the architect's one major departure from the classic. Lillie Hitchcock was a society belle of the 1880's who flouted the decorous customs of the period and was particularly noted for her habit of chasing fire wagons in her red shoes and helmet. At the sound of the bell she would not hesitate to desert a partner on the dance floor to dash off to the scene of the alarm—on horseback. When she died in the 1920's, (having married Howard Coit meantime) she left a sum of money to be devoted to a memorial to the city's volunteer fire fighters—which was erected in Washington Square—and another sum to be spent for "beautification of the city." Officials decided that the best use of the funds would be for construction of a building in the city park on top of Telegraph Hill, and they left the design to Brown.

It may be that the architect felt he could not do violence to the memory of the unorthodox Mrs. Coit by designing a conventional structure of any kind. Whatever his reasons, his design for Coit Tower was so unlike any of his previous work that it took the community by surprise. When completed in 1933 the shaft bore no resemblance to a Renaissance tower and had no classic precedent. Brown's taste was not completely shared by some admirers of his earlier works, and a quarter of a century later some old-timers were still referring derisively to the tower as "that silo." But the simple cylindrical fluted column has come to be generally accepted as one of the most distinctive marks on the city's skyline. It seems evidence that even the most confirmed traditionalist may sometimes recognize the demands of the times and the place for a decisive break with tradition.

One of the Civic Center buildings that do not bear the identifying marks of Brown's sure touch for the classic is the architecturally controversial city library. Its designer was George W. Kelham, a New Yorker who had been sent west by his firm for the reconstruction of the Palace Hotel after 1906, remained to open an office of his own, and eventually designed more major downtown buildings than any other single architect. The library, finished in 1917, was his first big job after the Palace, and in its adherence to tradition prefigures some of his skyscrapers. The Italian Renaissance structure has been praised as conveying a "scholarly atmosphere" and damned as belonging to the "Grand Central bahnhof school of library architecture." Possibly in order to avoid detracting from the "scholarly atmosphere" provided by the design, most of the library's books were consigned to hidden stacks inaccessible to the reader.

Most of Kelham's work was done during San Francisco's great decade of skyscraper building, the affluent Twenties. As the city's most successful commercial architect of the period, Kelham followed the lead of New York and Chicago architects in trying to make skyscrapers look as much as possible like Roman temples and Gothic cathedrals. His architectural signature is visible in all parts of the downtown area—on the Medico-Dental Building at 490 Post, the Federal Reserve Bank on Sansome, the California Commercial Union Building on Montgomery, and on the city's first genuine skyscraper, the Standard Oil Building, completed in 1921. The gray granite structure rises eighteen stories above the street relatively unadorned before reaching a flaring battlement. Then it suddenly seems to begin all over again with a massive façade of Doric columns several stories high, surmounted by a steep tile roof.

The second of Kelham's skyscrapers was the Russ Building, a block away, completed in 1927 on a piece of ground that Christian Russ had purchased from the city eighty years earlier for $37.50. For this thirty-one-story general office building Kelham decided to use a Gothic motif, which he maintained even to such details as the large niches at the Montgomery Street entrance, copies of those which in Gothic cathedrals held figures of the saints. Kelham's niches, however, remain empty.

Although Kelham's monumental buildings were widely praised, there was a strong minority dissent. The most emphatic voice raised against them, and against the prevailing downtown architecture of the Twenties, was that of the same Irving F. Morrow, who had earlier hailed Polk's revolutionary Hallidie Building.

"Our college courses," Morrow wrote, "tell us that architecture symbolizes the history and currents of thought of its age. Does it? What is there in these buildings that is at all contemporaneous? . . . There has not been a single example of an effort to escape forms long ago developed for cut stone, and seek fresher expression derived from the new medium of execution. Throughout their composition and handling they are subservient to past structural and decorative ideals."

In the later Twenties there were beginnings of a wider recognition of the point Morrow was making. Even Kelham, like Brown, showed toward the end of his career an awareness of the fact that old styles may not be completely adequate to the changing times. In his final skyscraper, the Shell Building, finished in 1929, it is possible to see signs of some departure from the purely traditional. The setback tower of the Shell Building, less self-consciously Gothic than the Russ Building, has strong vertical lines, and the

Telephone Buildi...

SHELL BUILDING
RUSS BUILDING
MARK HOPKINS HOTEL

*Buildings
on skyline:*

SHELL   ZELLERBACH   STANDARD   EQUITABLE   RUSS   DE YOUNG   CENTRAL

decorative work near the top takes advantage of the California sun, allowing the play of light and shadow on the sculptured walls to change with the time of day. When the building is illuminated at night by amber floodlights, it is the most striking feature of the city's skyline, looming above the darkened business district like a tower of glowing gold.

The city's search for architectural identity is illustrated best in the career of the last of the "big four" architects of the downtown skyline. Timothy Pfleuger was a hearty extrovert who combined business sagacity with artistic talent and an ability to draw out the best in those who worked for him. He was still in his early thirties when he was awarded the job of designing the head office of the Pacific Telephone and Telegraph Company—largest firm headquarters in the West. In his early sketches for the building he experimented with Gothic styles in the approved fashion but was not satisfied with them. Then he saw the plan for what was probably the most famous skyscraper ever designed—but never built. The plan had been submitted by the Finnish architect Eliel Saarinen in a competition for a design for the Chicago Tribune Building, but it was so radical a departure that it lost the Tribune competition to a conventional Gothic design. Saarinen's building was an aspiring form that reflected no traditional style but seemed to embody the very idea of a skyscraper—and of a skyscraper civilization. It fired Pfleuger's imagination; he designed a building in the Saarinen style and was elated when the proposal was accepted. In its refusal to copy classic styles the Telephone Building, finished in 1925, was the first architecturally modern skyscraper in San Francisco and one of the first in the nation.

Unlike the city's earlier high buildings, it has no horizontal lines; it does not try to disguise its form with cornices, buttresses, or gingerbread but accepts and accentuates its height with sharply ascending piers and tapering step-backs. The façade's decorations, suggestive of modern communication, illustrate well the idea that architecture is frozen music; a theme first stated in tentative form near the base of the building—a series of stemlike bas-reliefs—is repeated higher up at intervals, each time with greater elaboration until it reaches a climax at the top in a grand architectural fortissimo.

The building so dominates the skyline south of Market that it was chosen to fly the Weather Bureau's storm-warning signals—red pennants by day and lanterns by night. At 435 feet above street level it is the second-tallest building in the city, edged out by the Russ Building, one foot higher.

The style was Saarinen's as much as it was Pfleuger's. Other than Polk's Hallidie Building, San Francisco did not yet have a downtown building that was genuinely original. But with Pfleuger's sharp break with the classic the first step had been taken.

The Telephone Building was as much of a triumph as Arthur Brown's City Hall had been a decade earlier. And just as Brown continued in the same tradition for the rest of his life—except for Coit Tower—so Pfleuger, encouraged by having successfully taken a chance, continued to experiment with new ideas. His career is marked by a remarkable number of "firsts," from the Top o' the Mark, which set a new and widely imitated style in bars, to the subterranean Union Square Garage, the model for later under-park garages. And he proved that he could work in a wide variety of styles from the modern classic of the Stock Exchange (notable for its liberal use of sculpture and of murals, for which he imported Diego Rivera) to the Doric style of the white Metropolitan Life Insurance Company headquarters on Nob Hill and the unadorned marble-front store of I. Magnin on Union Square.

Pfleuger's greatest contribution to the city's skyline was the extraordinary medical building named simply by its address—450 Sutter. Here at last indigenous forms and ideas were put to use. One was an adaptation of the point Willis Polk had illustrated with his glass wall—that a steel frame building need not have massive walls. Pfleuger eliminated the heavy walls and set the windows at the outer rim of the building. He even carried the idea further with an adaptation of an old San Francisco tradition—the bay window. All of the building's windows are slightly bayed, and the bay effect is achieved with "wrap-around" windows at the building's corners, in the exact place that architects had always insisted must show massive strength in masonry.

The result was a building not only impressive from the outside but pleasant to use as well. The bayed windows flood the rooms with light and provide maximum views of the city's panoramas. The exterior is a tapestry of con-

450 Sutter

trasting textures; shining bands of glass, reflecting the sun, alternate with a textured Mayan design between the floors. Lighter-colored piers extending without interruption to the roof give the building a powerful vertical thrust. Further innovations were a roof-top solarium and a basement garage accommodating one thousand cars. (Unfortunately later architects did not follow Pfleuger's lead in the latter respect, a failure that contributed greatly to today's downtown traffic congestion.) Although 450 Sutter was criticized on minor points, its striking originality seemed evidence that architecturally the city was at last coming of age and establishing its own identity.

It turned out, however, that 450 Sutter was not the beginning of an era but the end of one. It was finished early in 1930 just a few months after the stock-market crash. Other tall buildings had risen on the skyline during the late Twenties—Hotels Mark Hopkins (1926) and Sir Francis Drake (1928) on Nob Hill, and several tall apartment houses on Russian Hill—but Pfleuger's vigorous glassy shaft on Sutter Street was the last large downtown building for a quarter of a century of depression and war.

Despite the dearth of downtown construction the 1930's provided the most striking features of the San Francisco skyline—the two great suspension bridges. More emphatically than any downtown buildings the bridges are San Franciscan. They copy nothing; they are modifications of nothing. Like all major structures they have predecessors whose principles they embody— in this case primarily the Brooklyn Bridge. But San Francisco's bridges went far beyond any others ever built—in size, in engineering achievement, in

*Bay Bridge
from the east*

Bay Bridge from
Yerba Buena Island

beauty, strength, and grace of form. Almost alone among the city's major structures, they seem to fulfill the promise of this city at the Western Gate.

The stories of the designing of both bridges vividly exemplify the conflict between the two forces shaping the city's skyline—the adherence to tradition and the impulse to create new forms. During the Twenties the traditional had usually won out. But in the Thirties new forces were emerging. In the development of the Bay Bridge design the opposing forces were appropriately represented by the two men who had become the symbols of those two influences at their best, Arthur Brown and Timothy Pfleuger. Both were members of the committee of consulting architects. The engineers who had developed the first designs had felt that their planned bridge was too starkly barren. In keeping with the notion that architecture is decoration, they added some "architecture"—various adornments and elaborations in the classic tradition, primarily on the piers, cable anchorages, and tunnel entrances.

Bay Bridge from Embarcadero

Brown, pleased with the classic influence, approved of the décor. The younger architect, fresh from his success with 450 Sutter, wanted instead to strip the decoration and restore the clean, unadorned, functional lines. Pfleuger, always an energetic salesman, succeeded in bringing the committee to his point of view, and Brown was outvoted. The adornments came off, and the bridge was completed in 1936 without so much as a gesture toward the classic tradition.

The design of the Golden Gate Bridge was the product of a similar conflict of philosophy. Joseph Strauss, the dynamic engineer who had carried on a twenty-year crusade on behalf of his lifetime ambition to bridge the Golden Gate, had some ideas about design that stemmed from deep roots in his personality. He was not necessarily committed to classic styles in the same sense that Arthur Brown was, but it sometimes happened that the classic seemed the best vehicle for his own tendencies toward flamboyance and display. In his preliminary design for the Golden Gate Bridge—an ungainly structure consisting of two cantilever spans connected by a suspension span—the bridge was adorned by a huge, ornately decorated entrance resembling the Arch of Triumph.

When the proposal to build the bridge was finally approved and the time came to go to work, Strauss wisely brought out from his Chicago office his assistant, Clifford E. Paine, a brilliant young hard-hat engineer with a personality that neatly complemented that of Strauss; he was willing to take charge of the engineering and leave the public relations to his boss. It was Strauss's zeal as a crusader that made it possible to build the bridge; it was Paine's engineering ability, his imagination, resourcefulness, and relentless drive that overcame a series of almost insuperable setbacks and got the bridge built.

As head of the engineering staff in Chicago, Paine had persuaded Strauss that his original design was impractical and had developed a design for a simple suspension bridge. The site itself determined many of the proportions, including the requirement of a span far longer than any ever constructed. As Paine and his staff worked out the basic engineering problems, the bridge began to take shape on paper—the height and proportions of the towers, the lengths of the center and side spans, the location of the cable anchorages, the curve of the cables, the height of the deck. Paine made a major decision to use open "portal" bracing for the stepped-back towers above the deck, rather than the more conventional X-type bracing used for the towers of the Bay Bridge. It is the portal bracing that gives the bridge much of its characteristic openness and spaciousness.

Golden Gate Bridge from Marin County

Golden Gate Bridge from the Presidio

Once the outline was set by Paine, an architect was called in to develop the details of appearance. Fittingly, the architect chosen was Irving F. Morrow—the same Morrow who had been almost alone in lauding Willis Polk's precedent-breaking Hallidie Building and who for years had condemned the lack of originality in most of San Francisco's downtown architecture. Morrow's uncompromising opposition to the imitation of traditional forms had been largely responsible for the fact that he had not found clients willing to hire him to design a single major building. But now Morrow was at last given the opportunity to demonstrate—on a colossal scale—the philosophy he had long been preaching.

Ironically, however, in collaborating with Paine on the architectural features of the design, Morrow sometimes found himself upholding a relatively conservative point of view. Paine's practical, no-nonsense attitude made him skeptical of all decoration. Morrow had never opposed decoration in itself but only the practice of imitating forms developed in earlier eras. He was able to convince Paine that some degree of decoration was desirable. The viewpoints of the two men (and to some degree of Mrs. Morrow, also an architect) were fused in the final design. Morrow's hand is visible in the details—in the upward-diminishing size of the portals, emphasizing the bridge's height; in the decorated steel plates hiding the skeleton steelwork of the braces over the deck; in the bridge's deep red color, complementing the colors of the rocks and cliffs; in the graceful arching lamps along the roadway; in the open rail, which permits automobile passengers to see the breathtaking view from the deck.

The open railing exemplifies a cardinal point of Morrow's philosophy— the principle that a structure of any kind should be designed not merely for its outward appearance but also for the convenience and aesthetic pleasure of those who use it. "What validity can be claimed," he once wrote, "for an evaluation of a people's art which fails to recognize its points of contact with the people and with the practical needs of everyday life? We must strive until all the amenities of an enlightened culture are accessible to every man by virtue of his dignity, his significance and his possibilities as a member of human society . . . Our architecture, like our democracy, must be a free expression from within outward . . ."

Crown-Zellerbach Building (CENTER); *Hobart Building* (EXTREME LEFT); *Standard Oil Building* (BEHIND CROWN-ZELLERBACH); *Shell Building* (UPPER RIGHT).

In the late 1950's, when San Francisco once again began building sky-scrapers after a lapse of a quarter century, there were indications that the philosophy expressed by Morrow was taking hold.

The architects seemed to consider not merely the monumental appearance of the buildings from a distance (usually the governing consideration of the older architects) but the comfort and aesthetic needs of the occupants—their access to light and air and view, "the practical needs of everyday life."

In many of the new buildings indigenous ideas of design seemed to be emerging over the older tendency merely to copy traditional styles. Although it took modern architecture forty years to catch up with him, Willis Polk would surely approve of the glassy new Crown-Zellerbach Building on Market Street (Hertzka and Knowles: and Skidmore, Owings and Merrill, associated architects), the direct descendant of his own original glass-curtain wall in the Hallidie Building.

A variation of Polk's curtain wall was developed for the vast new Bank of America Building at Market and Van Ness (Wurster, Bernardi and Emmons, architects). Instead of glass, the curtain walls are composed of huge concrete panels hauled from the factory to the site and bolted into place, forming the earthquake and wind bracing for the building.

Doubtless Polk himself would be out in front again, designing buildings forty years ahead of our own time. The new era of skyscraper building in San Francisco is yet too young to indicate whether most of its architects will tend to imitate the new skyscrapers of New York or develop the full potential of indigenous Western ideas and forms. With a world of possibil-ities before them, the new architects might well ponder San Francisco's search for identity—a search written on the skyline from the Ferry Building, symbol of the past, to the two great bridges, which seem to thrust vigorously toward a limitless future.

Richmond-San Rafael Bridge

Sunset District

Sausalito

Nob Hill; Sacramento Street

Near McLaren Park

*Sutro Heights,
near Cliff House*

*Portsmouth Plaza;
Kearny Street*

Telegraph Hill from Russian Hill

CHAPTER III

The Neighborhoods

Start with Telegraph Hill—near the city's beginnings.

To see the hill properly, go on foot. Climb the high-angled streets and the long flights of steps and wander slowly over the steep upper slopes.

The first thing you notice is the light—a dazzling incandescence that flashes up from below through the eucalyptus trees and floods in through the windows of houses, illuminating walls and ceilings.

It comes from below because you are half surrounded—on the north and east—by an inverted sky, the luminous surface of San Francisco Bay, which reflects the sun, the clouds, and the bright summer fogs that flow in through the Golden Gate. And you are half surrounded—on the south and west—by the city itself, another source of radiance, for San Francisco, even more literally than Paris, is a city of light. Its massed buildings, sweeping upward in steep crescendos on hills above the bay, seem almost entirely white, bleached and burnished by the perennial salt winds from the ocean.

It is fitting that the brilliance of the city and bay seem to come to intense focus here, for Telegraph Hill is in many ways the focus of San Francisco itself; it has been the city's Acropolis and its Parnassus, its Left Bank and Hyde Park, the sum and quintessence of the city's uniqueness and diversity. In a city of hills rising suddenly in the middle of a block, of streets taking off at crazy angles for the sky above or the bay below, of a heterogeneous people with a traditional fondness for the bizarre and eccentric, Telegraph Hill is by far the steepest, most bizarre, heterogeneous, and eccentric sector of all.

There are hillside streets so narrow a car can scrape fenders on both sides; others so steep they are closed to automobiles entirely. There are lanes, officially labeled as streets, that are simply paths or steps through the trees between overgrown geranium gardens and houses spilling dizzily down precipitous slopes. There is a crazy-quilt mélange of residents representing nearly every element of the city's populace. The landlord from Genoa, for example, has lived on the hill for half a century but seldom finds a need to use his two-dozen words of English; his neighbor just across the lane is a well-to-do building contractor who emigrated at an early age from his native Canton; the grocer down the hill was born in some undetermined part of the Far East and communicates with customers effectively in his own ingenious pidgin English; the barber on Union Street was born in Cádiz; the nearby launderette owner was a Silesian refugee from nazi concentration camps and used to manage an American club in Manila.

Along Grant Avenue near the foot of the hill's western slope are three or four of the most intriguing blocks in the city. There are Italian shops, cafés, and ravioli factories; Chinese laundries and sewing rooms; shops of artisans —ceramists, weavers, leatherworkers, metalsmiths; tiny art galleries and the dark bistros of the city's current crop of bohemians. There is the Trieste Coffee House, the Latin American printery, and the Hawaiian Luahala Room. The street swarms with tiny yelling Chinese children, old Italian women in shawls, bearded bohemians—Caucasian, Oriental, and Negro— and baggy-clothed youths hoping to be taken for members of the mythical Beat Generation.

The hill's buildings are as diverse as its population, ranging from aged cottages, of the type that once lodged such bohemians as Robert Louis Stevenson, Edwin Booth, George Sterling, and Jack London, to the glassy apartments inhabited by the junior executives and professional people who have invaded large areas of the hill's Parnassian heights. Whatever their age, most of the dwellings have one quality in common—they are permeated with the flavor of the city. Living here, you are close to the pulse of San Francisco.

Before you are fully awake in the morning, the privacy of your sleep is invaded by the sounds of the ships that have anchored in the bay during the night and are now heading for the docks, their whistle blasts echoing resonantly from the city's hills. Out the window, just beyond your breakfast

Telegraph Hill; Fresno and Kearn

Telegraph Hill; Fresno near Grant

Telegraph Hill; the east side

coffeepot, you may see the old windjammer *Balclutha* spreading her spars against a backdrop of the bay's blues and greens. You may look up from your morning newspaper to watch a load of Volkswagens swinging over the rail of a black freighter from Hamburg, a giant flat-top moving ponderously toward the Golden Gate with a helicopter practicing landings on her deck, a fleet of fishing boats hovering over a school of striped bass off Alcatraz.

The sound of your vacuum cleaner fails to drown out the rumble and clang of the Belt Line Railroad shunting freight cars to and from the ships at the piers, and the music of your phonograph is often accompanied by a foghorn obbligato. You can gaze out the window and watch the changes in weather moving across the bay to the far shores, observe a rainstorm in Richmond or a fog bank over Sausalito or the sun in Berkeley or even the snow on Mount St. Helena, sixty miles to the north.

In the summertime you can see a long arm of fog flow in through the

Columbus Avenue, Mount Tamalpais

Golden Gate, billow up in translucent domes over the bay's islands, creep up the hill to swirl outside your door and press against the windowpanes. In the winter, when the north winds sweep down from Carquinez across the blue expanse of water, flecking it with whitecaps, the windows rattle, the building shakes in the blast, and you can watch the struggles of the tugboats against the gale and the straining of the ships at their lines. The gulls wheel past your window, the tides run swiftly below, the rhythms of the city and the bay become the rhythms of everyday living.

Long before the completion of Coit Tower, in 1933, the hill's summit had been a lookout and gathering place for generations of San Franciscans. During the Gold Rush a semaphore on that spot, connected by telegraph to a lookout at Point Lobos, seven miles away, signaled to the city below the news of the arrival of each ship off the Golden Gate, sending the populace swarming to the hill to cheer the vessel's arrival.

The Gold Rush city was located on Yerba Buena Cove, just south of the hill, and the skyscrapers of today's financial district are built on piles over the filled-in harbor where the Forty-Niners anchored. Hundreds of sailing vessels were abandoned in the cove when their crews headed for the Mother Lode, and some of their hulls still can be found beneath present-day buildings. The edge of the old cove was along the line of Montgomery Street, and nearby Portsmouth Plaza was the nucleus from which the city spread over the hills.

North Beach; Columbus and Broadway

To the west, in the narrow valley between Telegraph and Russian Hills, is a community as heterogeneous in some ways as Telegraph Hill itself. Guidebooks refer to the neighborhood as the Latin Quarter, but to San Franciscans it has always been North Beach (although there is no beach in sight nowadays)—home of pizza, balladeers, bohemians, and bars featuring grand opera. Along the bottom of the valley is North Beach's main street, Columbus Avenue, which begins at what was once the edge of old Yerba Buena Cove and cuts diagonally northwest across the grid of the other streets, creating odd-shaped "islands" and odder-shaped buildings. It passes through an area of such off-beat night clubs as the Hungry I and the Purple Onion, crosses Broadway with its cafés and bars of a dozen nationalities, proceeds through a sector where the store signs read "Buon Gusto" and "L'Italia" and the spoken accents are those of Lucca and Genoa, reaches a high point near the church of St. Francis of Assisi, and descends past Washington Square into a picture-frame view of the bay, Sausalito, and Mount Tamalpais rising half a mile into the sky.

Columbus crosses Bay Street at the site of the vanished beach from which the community takes its name. The shore line of the cove, now several blocks inland from Fisherman's Wharf, curved from here to the foot of Telegraph Hill; an old house still standing on Midway Street once belonged to a fisherman who used to tie up his boat near the building, now four blocks from the waterfront.

Most of North Beach was destroyed by fire in 1906, and its residential buildings are characteristic of the immediate postfire era—two- and three-story wooden flats painted white or gray; nearly all of them bulge out over the sidewalks with the traditional San Francisco bay window. This type of window first developed centuries ago in medieval buildings to enable the inhabitants to see whether friend or enemy was at the front door, a purpose it still serves for San Francisco housewives. It achieved a particular efflorescence here for other reasons, however. In this crowded, often foggy city the bay window reaches out for all possible space and light and for the omnipresent views of hills or water at the ends of the streets.

In San Francisco the bay window is an art form. Each housebuilder seemed to take a craftsman's pride in developing variations on the theme,

Bay windows

*Bay
windows*

with the imaginative use of angles, curves, and ornamentation. Occasionally, in adjacent buildings, the urge to bulge has outdone itself, and each resident's principal view is into the living room of his next-door neighbor.

In the days before the great fire Russian Hill, like Telegraph, was scattered with the cottages of the bohemians. But with more level area at the top than Telegraph, it was also the site of Victorian mansions surrounded by landscaped gardens. A few remain, such as three big houses built in the 1860's now hidden in groves of trees near the top of Chestnut Street. One of them, the Spring House at 944 Chestnut, has a name with a double significance; it was owned for half a century by the Francis Spring family and originally was surrounded by a moat to protect it from the natural water welling up out of the ground. Among its other distinctions it was for a time the home of Bruce Porter, an eminent landscape architect and painter who designed many of the palatial gardens of estates down the San Francisco Peninsula. His wife was the daughter of philosopher William James, and for many years the Porters made the Spring House a kind of salon for the city's intellectuals. More recently it has housed ski master Hannes Schroll.

On Green Street between Jones and Leavenworth, in a block of attractively maintained houses about a century old, is a curious octagonal house built in 1858, remnant of a fad of the Fifties. A couple of blocks away, at 1032 Broadway, stands the oldest home on the hill. It was built in 1853 by a contractor named Atkinson, who made his money—or a good part of it—constructing the prison buildings at San Quentin. The clapboard walls of the house were covered with plaster about 1900, and as a result it appears relatively modern on the exterior; its age is betrayed only by its narrow windows.

Russian Hill's mansions are disappearing as rapidly as Telegraph Hill's cottages. The larger area of this hill and its superb views made it irresistible to the builders of skyscraper apartment houses, and the tall slim buildings are Russian Hill's characteristic mark on the skyline. The big apartments have not yet completely obliterated the hill's original flavor, however; there are still some quiet precincts on the hillsides where even automobiles are still barred. The atmosphere of earlier eras lingers along overgrown Macondray Lane, for example, and on the steep paths along Vallejo above

Russian Hill, looking no

Mason. The hill's most unique street accessible to automobiles is Lombard, which zigzags down the east slope in a series of landscaped switchbacks, reputedly the crookedest street in the world (although it is closely rivaled by Vermont Street on Potrero Hill).

Russian Hill is the northern part of a ridge that reaches a high point at Vallejo Street, dips down to the south into a saddle occupied by Pacific Avenue (which was once the pass leading to the "wilderness" in the west), and rises again as Nob Hill. Despite the fire of 1906, which leveled most of the hill's buildings, there is still visible evidence of the "nabobs" for whom Nob Hill was supposedly named and who built their garish palaces here in the 1860's and '70's. One such piece of evidence is the California Street cable line, built by the railroad titans—Stanford, Huntington, Hopkins, and Crocker—for easy access to their commanding heights. Another is the old retaining wall surrounding the block occupied by the Mark Hopkins Hotel and the Stanford Court Apartments. The wall was built by Stanford and Hopkins around their adjacent residences and is composed of leftover granite blocks they had used in building the transcontinental railroad through the Sierra Nevada at Donner Pass. The old brownstone Pacific Union Club is also in part a remnant of the prefire era; it occupies the site and the walls of the fire-gutted mansion of silver-king James Flood. Next door is a park on the site of the Huntington house; the Crocker mansion was across the street where Grace Cathedral now stands.

The Fairmont Hotel, built on property that once belonged to James Fair, another of the silver kings, is in part also a remnant of the prefire era. It was just approaching completion in April of 1906 and was gutted by the fire, but its walls were used in the restoration. The designer of the interior was the nation's most famous architect of the period, Stanford White, a New York epicure and *bon vivant* whose tastes are reflected in the hotel's classic lines and décor. The Fairmont proved to be the capstone of White's career. The hotel's reconstruction was barely under way when he was killed in the roof-top night club at Madison Square Garden by Harry Thaw, jealous husband of glamour girl Evelyn Nesbit, with whom White had carried on an affair.

Near the crest of the hill, at the intersection of Jones and Clay, rises the twenty-story Clay-Jones Apartments, the highest in elevation (although not the tallest) downtown building in San Francisco. Its two-story penthouse is literally the top abode in the city. On the roof is the radio transmitter of station KCBS, rising 650 feet above the bay.

Russian Hill; Union Street

Nob Hill; Pacific Union Club

On the south Nob Hill slopes down into the valley occupied by Market Street. When City Engineer Jasper O'Farrell in 1847 drew on his map a line representing a street to be known as Market; his main purpose was to lay out a new road paralleling the old trail heading southwest from the village at Yerba Buena Cove to Mission Dolores. The fact that, to do so, he had to plot Market on a fifty-four-degree diagonal seemed unimportant at the time. But when the north-south streets at the village were extended through to Market in later years, the consequences were staggering—triangular-shaped blocks, giving migraine to building designers, and intersections where four separate streets converge at odd angles, creating a no man's land willingly entered only by the foolhardy.

Nob Hill; California Stree

I. MAGNIN & CO.

North of Market; opposite Union Square

South of Market;
Howard Street

Doubtless O'Farrell did not realize, either, as he drew the line of Market on his map, that he was creating a future social cleavage in the city. The fashionable shopping, financial, and hotel districts north of the city's main thoroughfare bear little resemblance to the area of industrial plants, whole-sale firms, cheap hotels, and flophouses in the section immediately south of Market. There is one characteristic the two sections have in common, how-ever. They are inhabited principally by unmarried people who live by them-selves. The lonely and the unhappy gravitate here, and these two areas are largely responsible for the city's disproportionately high number of alcohol-ics and suicides. (Because of San Francisco's geographic isolation the statis-tics are often misleading; figures for the entire Bay Area include a more nor-mal proportion of family neighborhoods to downtown areas and are thus much closer to the national average.)

Much of the skid-row area south of Market, now a Slough of Despond for many of its inhabitants, was once a real slough adjoining a good-sized cove known as Mission Bay. A lagoon originally extended from the cove inward about two miles from the present bay shore and covered the central part of the present-day Mission District.

The Mission District is actually a valley enclosed on three sides by hills that shelter it from fog and wind and enable its residents to claim the city's best climate. The valley's ideal location caused Juan Bautista de Anza in 1776 to choose it for the site of Mission San Francisco de Asís, which became known as Mission Dolores because it was located on a creek flowing down Arroyo de los Dolores to the lagoon.

In the 1860's and '70's, long before the district was a residential area, its big attraction was Woodward's Gardens, a kind of nineteenth-century Disneyland, with playgrounds, landscaped gardens, a museum, an aquarium, seal ponds, and such breath-taking demonstrations as giant balloon ascents. Block-long Woodward Street, off Mission at Fourteenth, still marks the lo-cation.

The Mission District's great period of growth began when the fire of 1906 burned out the old "working class" districts south of Market and many of its inhabitants moved west into the valley of Mission Dolores. Long known as the stronghold of the city's Irish population, the Mission now also con-

Mission District; Mission Park

tains a Spanish-speaking colony centered around Twenty-fourth Street. The entire district is characterized by fierce local pride, a shopping district second in size only to that of Market Street, and a Mission accent that thus far has baffled linguistic experts. The more chauvinistic Missionites traditionally brag that they would never be caught dead north of Market.

Potrero Hill, rising between the Mission and the bay, and now divided from the Mission by the Bayshore Freeway, resembles the Mission in its rather plain frame houses and is the home of a comparable income group, but it has some distinctions of its own. It possesses sweeping views of the downtown area and the bay; it has fewer boardinghouses and a higher proportion of families than the Mission; it includes a larger foreign-born popu-

Potrero Hill

lation, particularly Russian; and it increasingly attracts artists and writers in flight from the gray-flannel-suit invasion of Telegraph Hill.

Architecturally far more intriguing than either the Mission or Potrero is the Western Addition—added to the city in the 1860's and often referred to simply as the "Fillmore," for its main street. Having escaped the great fire, the houses of the district are generally the oldest in the city. They are the famed Victorian gingerbread or "carpenter Gothic" houses—museum pieces of an era when the search for beauty took some strange turns. Most of them were constructed during the 1870's and '80's, many in tract-house blocks. Reacting to the stark functional simplicity of the earlier pioneer period, builders went to the opposite extreme and tried to incorporate in smaller houses the architectural flamboyance that had previously been found in the

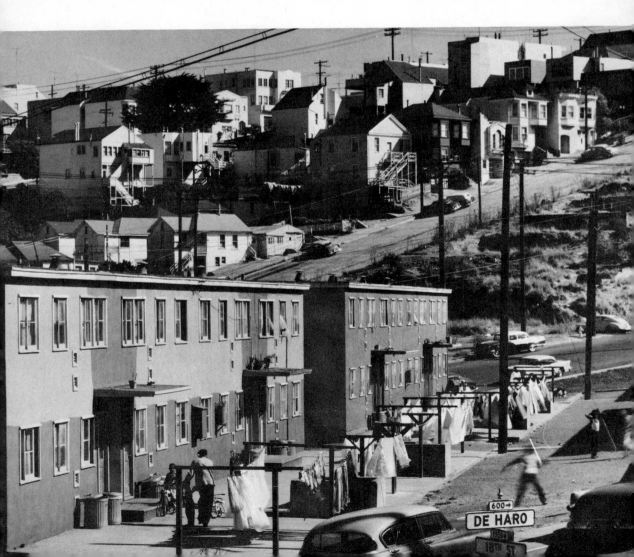

Western Addition; California Street

gaudier saloons and the mansions of Nob Hill and that reached a climax in William Ralston's Palace Hotel with its four hundred bay windows.

The houses of the Western Addition have bay windows in startling proliferation. With basically similar floor plans they have façades that are fantastic elaborations of gables, cornices, arches, turrets, and columns copied from a half-dozen architectural periods—decorated like a wedding cake with intricate scrollwork ad infinitum, all within the limitations of a twenty-five-foot lot. There was no pretense of originality; the scrollwork designs could easily be ordered by the yard from the catalogues of lumber mills whose jigsaws were busily turning them out by the mile. Countless redwood trees in California's northern forests were ignominiously reduced to wooden lace embroidery designed to lure buyers of Western Addition tract houses.

In 1906 the business district along Fillmore boomed furiously for a few months as the successor to burned-out Market Street but soon returned to normal as the downtown area was rebuilt. By the beginning of World War II many of the old houses in the area had already begun to fall apart. To accommodate the influx of warworkers, many of them Negroes from impoverished areas of the South, the old places were divided inside into tiny flats, apartments, and furnished rooms. Inevitable overcrowding and lack of upkeep caused them to deteriorate further, and the core of the Western Addition became a seriously blighted area with high priority on the city's plans for slum clearance and redevelopment.

Some of the old houses, however, particularly in the fringe areas, have been scrupulously maintained. Artistically painted and refurbished, they are fashionable residences of business and professional people who take as much pride in their period pieces as do the fanciers of Chippendale furniture or Stutz-Bearcats. A half-dozen such houses on Clay Street opposite Alta Plaza have an added interest; they were mail-order houses, constructed in Chicago in the 1870's, shipped to San Francisco in parts, and assembled on the site—"prefabs" long before the term was coined.

To the north of the Western Addition is Pacific Heights, an area as architecturally diverse as the Western Addition is uniform. Like a cutaway hillside that reveals geologic strata of different epochs, the houses of Pacific

'estern Addition "mansions"

Heights are residues of various eras of the city's growth. One of the earliest eras is represented in the big Queen Anne-style frame houses of the 1880's and '90's; their most distinguishing features are gabled roofs and a corner tower bulging with bay windows and often topped by an observation room (a style exemplified elsewhere in the older houses around Buena Vista Park).

Dating from the later 1890's are the brick or brownstone mansions such as the old Whittier house at Jackson and Laguna, present home of the California Historical Society. This house is an architectural showpiece if only for its ornate interior. Just before World War II it housed the German Consulate; Government agents moving in after Pearl Harbor found the ashes of consular documents in the fireplaces, a big telescope in the tower to observe ship movements in the bay, and a short-wave radio transmitter.

Pacific Heights; Adolph B. Spreckels house

Latter-day nabobs who were burned off Nob Hill in 1906 moved west to Pacific Heights and built here houses considerably more tasteful than most of the garish palaces consumed in the fire. Among them is the white Corinthian mansion of Adolph and Alma Spreckels on Lafayette Square, built in 1913 with a fortune made in the sugar trade, and the big house in the next block erected five years later by James D. Phelan, socialite attorney, turn-of-the-century mayor of San Francisco and later California's United States senator. The city's other wealthy families built homes indulging their own tastes in styles traditionally symbolic of prestige and respectability— Corinthian classic, brick Georgian, gabled Tudor, tile-roofed Spanish, and variations thereon.

In the 1920's, with a great population increase, a new development came to Pacific Heights; six- and eight-story luxury apartment houses began to replace aging frame mansions, particularly in the older eastern end of the district.

Some of the old houses were remodeled inside into apartments and others became schools. The $3,000,000 château built on Broadway near Fillmore by James L. Flood, son of the silver king, and the Joseph D. Grant home next door are now schools operated by the Convent of the Sacred Heart. Still others, in the period during and after World War II, gave birth to a notable San Francisco institution—the guesthouse.

Bearing little resemblance to the old-fashioned boardinghouse, the guesthouses are inhabited largely by young business and professional people who come to San Francisco from other parts of the country and enjoy a full social life in the crowded old mansions. Many a former millionaire's residence is now the scene of far greater social activity than it ever housed in the days of grand receptions, debuts, and formal balls. The white classic Rudolph Spreckels house at Pacific and Gough, its interior still resplendent with Italian marble, was converted into the Colonial Residence Club; the lavish home of cattle baron Henry Miller at Laguna and Clay became the Park Manor Residence Club; and the Rothschild mansion at Jackson and Gough became the central house of the Château Bleu, composed of several of the nearby houses under the same management. The guesthouse has already become one of the institutions that best maintain San Francisco's reputation as a city of friendliness and congeniality.

Despite the advent of apartments and guesthouses in the eastern sectors of Pacific Heights, the western end of the district, (which becomes Presidio Heights where it adjoins the army post,) is still pre-eminently an area of one-family homes and three-Cadillac garages. There the oldest of the houses are being replaced not by apartments but by modern homes with glass walls overlooking the Golden Gate. One example is the big redwood house at Washington and Maple designed by the German architect Eric Mendelsohn. Mendelsohn habitually sought inspiration by playing Bach's architectonic fugues on the phonograph while he worked, but although the building may have been inspired by the eighteenth-century composer, it is strictly twentieth-century in design.

At the foot of the steep northern slope of Pacific Heights is an area that was responsible for quenching the thirst of early-day San Franciscans in two different ways—both harmless. As a source of the city's water in the early 1850's the eastern end of the district, closest to Van Ness Avenue, was known as Spring Valley. Farther west, closer to the Presidio, was a dairy area known as Cow Hollow. Springs issuing from the foot of Pacific Heights flowed through both areas toward the bay, but before reaching it their waters collected in ponds behind high sand dunes along the shore. The largest of the ponds was Washerwoman's Lagoon around the area of Filbert and Franklin. The washerwomen disappeared when the lagoon began to reek from the sewage of a tannery on its shores and was subsequently filled in. One of the springs still flows, however—in the garden of St. Mary the Virgin Episcopal Church at Union and Steiner—and served once again as a source of water in 1906 when the earthquake broke the water mains.

Cow Hollow, which once fronted on the sand dunes of the bay shore, was left high and dry when the cove between Fort Mason and the Presidio was filled in for the Panama-Pacific International Exposition of 1915. The district's commercial center along Union Street boomed expansively during the exposition, and Cow Hollow merchants were optimistic about the economic benefits of a new subdivision scheduled to rise on the exposition grounds after the fair was over. But their hopes did not pan out. City officials were not sure whether to zone the bayside area for residential or industrial

Presidio Heights; Leon Russell house by Mendelsoh

Presidio Heights; the Presidio wall

and harbor purposes. Exposition lovers insisted that some of the fair buildings be retained, and park enthusiasts felt that the area should be planted with greenery.

The solution was designed to make everybody happy. Half of the waterfront area was allotted to a yacht harbor, or marina, from which the district took its name; the other half was to be planted to lawn for a park. The exposition's magnificent Palace of Fine Arts would be left standing and the bulk of the area zoned for housing. But even after streets were put in, the expected rush to occupy the Marina failed to materialize. After the glitter and glamour of the exposition, these weedy, windy wastes, broken only by a few forlorn trees and decaying monuments of the fair, were unappealing to potential residents. The park—the Marina Green—and the yacht harbor were slow in developing, and it was not until a dozen years after the exposition closed that new buildings began to mushroom on the flat sandy tract. Most of the Marina was built up in the five or six years of the late 1920's and early '30's.

The landscaped grace and spaciousness of the exposition had little impact on the builders, who felt that the most profitable types of dwellings would be solid rows of flats and small apartment houses, built flush with the sidewalk, with the legal minimum of yards in back. The façades were decorated in the prevailing mode of the era—the years when the senior Douglas Fairbanks was in his balcony-hopping prime; Rudolph Valentino on his white horse galloped across thousands of movie screens; and there was a nationwide pursuit of all things romantic. The architecture of romance was Spanish, and much of the Marina displays its distinguishing characteristics, the tile roof, white stucco, lacy ironwork, and arched windows and doorways. Even the Marina's street names carry out the Spanish motif—Cervantes, Alhambra, Toledo, Mallorca.

Some of the romantic tendencies of the same period are found on a grander scale in the city's few districts of homes that are expensive enough to justify lawns and gardens on this crowded peninsula—areas such as Forest Hill and St. Francis Wood, west of Twin Peaks, and Sea Cliff, overlooking the outer Golden Gate.

The Marina

Marina, Cow Hollow, Pacific Heights

West of the central ridge of hills, which divides the peninsula—from Mount Davidson to Twin Peaks to the Presidio—the entire aspect of the city changes. The sharp diversities of topography, social composition, and architecture that characterize the areas of the eastern slope are here toned down, muted, leveled off. The principal cause of the leveling off is the ocean, which for millenniums has been battering away at the coastal cliffs south of San Francisco, grinding them into sand, and depositing the sand along Ocean Beach. The sea wind has picked up the sand from the beach and distributed it impartially all over the western slope, filling valleys, submerging hills in deep drifts, and creating the area known in the early days as the Great Sand Waste.

When in the decades around the turn of the century the area was bisected with the green swath of Golden Gate Park, proving that the conquest of the dunes was possible, settlers began cautiously to edge westward between the park and the Presidio. The first line of advance was along the old Point Lobos toll road, which led to the city's famed early-day resort, the Cliff House. The road was later named for John W. Geary, the city's first American mayor, and became the main street of the new district. Residents who were not happy to be known as inhabitants of the Great Sand Waste decided that the district needed a name of some distinction and settled on "Richmond."

Often called Park-Presidio or simply the "Avenues," the Richmond District is today predominantly the home of small businessmen, clerical and supervisory employees, and an occasional family of middle-class Chinese and Negroes who can afford to live outside Chinatown and the Fillmore area. The houses of the neighborhood reflect several eras. Along the streets of the inner Richmond, among the newer apartment houses, remain some of the "carpenter Gothic" dwellings of the 1870's and '80's. Farther west, frame or stucco flats with turn-of-the-century décor give way to the Spanish styles of the 1920's.

Different as it is from the eastern areas of the city, the Richmond is nevertheless unmistakably San Franciscan. Drive down long treeless blocks of wall-to-wall flats and suddenly, rising to the top of a built-over sand dune, you are confronted with a breath-taking view of ocean or hills or a startling glimpse of the red towers of the Golden Gate Bridge.

The area south of Golden Gate Park was still mainly sand dunes for decades after the Richmond was a thriving community. As early as 1887 an ambitious real estate developer tried to hold the drifts with great quantities of red rock from a quarry on Mount Sutro. He named the area the Sunset District and hopefully started a community along the eastern edge of the dunes. But the winds still blew across miles of open sand, drifting it against the new buildings and for nearly another half century the Sunset was little more than a few frame houses huddled along Irving and Judah streets. Then, in the 1930's, the dunes met their match—a Dutch builder named Henry Doelger, who decided that the only way to conquer the sand was to do it wholesale.

The Richmond; George Washington High School

To make the kind of all-out assault he planned, Doelger knew that he would have to build houses that would sell quickly. He shrewdly realized that the greatest market lay in the masses of families who wanted homes of their own but could not afford the normal price of a separate house. His solution was a row house of a kind never before built on such a scale. On twenty-five-foot lots he raised block after block of white wall-to-wall houses that were basically identical but attempted to give each owner a feeling of individuality by applying various façades. The buyer could pay his few dollars monthly and take his choice of styles, none of which was exactly duplicated in the same block. In front of each house, further bolstering the buyer's pride as a landowner, was a tiny plot of grass and a few shrubs.

Despite the district's inevitable uniformity (which has caused critics to refer caustically to "the white cliffs of Doelger,") most Sunset residents infinitely prefer their neighborhood to the city's older districts. They carry on a spirited rivalry with residents of the Richmond District, whom they resemble in income and social status. Sunseters are principally first-generation San Franciscans and tend to regard the Richmondites as mossbacks, while the latter, often second- and third-generation, look condescendingly on the Sunseters as immigrants.

Although the Sunset and the outer Richmond are often referred to as the fog belt, the term is appropriate only during the summer months. On many a winter day, when the inner areas of the city are blanketed with a thick tule fog, both the Sunset and the Richmond, warmed by the ocean currents, bask in brilliant sunshine.

From Telegraph Hill to the Sunset—and to the smaller districts that spill over the city's southern hills from Parkmerced to Candlestick Cove—is a considerable distance geographically and an even greater distance architecturally and sociologically. To anyone exploring the neighborhoods in search of the city's identity the contrasts offer perplexing questions. Is Telegraph

The Sunset

Hill actually more "San Franciscan" than the Sunset—or do San Franciscans simply like to think so? Are the long rows of white tract houses in the Sunset any less characteristic of the city than the rows of traditionally San Franciscan carpenter Gothic tract houses of the Western Addition?

The answers are not yet clear. San Francisco's elusive identity must be sought not only in the neighborhoods but in many other aspects of the city's life.

Sunset Reservoir

University of California, Berkeley

Corona Heights, near Buena Vista

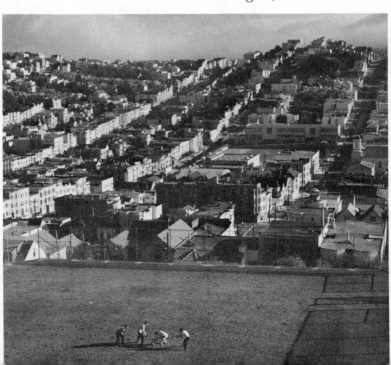

Telegraph Hill; Christopher Columbus

Russian Hill; Broadway

Howard Street

Nob Hill; Clay-Jones apartments

Nob Hill; California Street

CHAPTER IV

Some San Franciscans

Just as the "typical" Londoner is a man with a bowler, an umbrella, a stiff upper lip, and a quiet passion for four-o'clock tea, so the "typical" San Franciscan has his own marks of identification. He is inevitably a conservatively dressed sophisticate who lives in Pacific Heights, works on Montgomery Street, reveres the cable cars, loves the city's drifting fogs, and is nostalgic about the old days of the ferries. He is not typical at all, of course, except in the city's mythology, but his type does constitute an important social stratum, and his mores and folkways are therefore significant to an understanding of San Francisco.

He may be a third- or fourth-generation San Franciscan who attended the Town School for Boys on Jackson Street (or one of its predecessors) and an Ivy League university or perhaps Stanford. While a member of the younger set, he centers his social and service activities around the Bachelors, the University Club, and the Guardsmen (who send underprivileged children to summer camp). On winter weekends he is apt to be seen around the ski lodges at Sugar Bowl or Squaw Valley, and he counts a summer as a total loss unless he spends several weekends at "the lake" (Tahoe). Eventually he is tapped for membership in at least one of the big clubs, perhaps the St. Francis Yacht Club or the San Francisco Golf Club or such downtown bastions of tradition as the Bohemian, Olympic, or Pacific Union clubs.

Traditionally apathetic about what goes on at the City Hall, he nevertheless has a strong sense of civic responsibility, which he discharges as a patron of one of the big art museums (the San Francisco Museum of Art, the M. H. de Young, or the Legion of Honor, or as a board or committee member of such organizations as the United Crusade, the Mental Health Association, the World Affairs Council, or the Commonwealth Club.

His wife will regularly rendezvous with her friends under the clock at the St. Francis Hotel and attend the traditional Monday luncheon there in the Mural Room. She probably sends her daughters to Miss Burke's School in Pacific Heights and to her own alma mater in the East (such as Vassar, Smith, or Wellesley), presents them at the proper age in the annual Debutante Cotillion at the Sheraton-Palace Hotel, and grooms them early for the Junior League and the Spinsters.

The "typical" San Francisco couple holds season tickets for the symphony, dines regularly in the Garden Court of the Sheraton-Palace, or at such other old-time institutions as Amelio's, the Blue Fox, Ernie's, or Jack's, and on Fridays at Fisherman's Wharf. They wouldn't miss an opening night at the opera, the beginning of an important stage attraction at the Curran or Geary, or the first night of a very-big-name night-club act as the Venetian Room of the Fairmont. Their social doings are regularly reported—with a note of awe—in the society pages, and their foibles are chronicled—with a dash of salt—by Herb Caen, the city's irreverent columnist laureate.

Although in the city's folklore they have become Mr. and Mrs. San Francisco, they are apt to know the city too well to claim a monopoly on the title. Actually the typical San Franciscan is just as likely to be a longshoreman who lives in the Mission District and never goes near the Opera House, a merchant with a small store in the Richmond who has yet to see the inside of the St. Francis, or a bank clerk from the outer Sunset who never goes to Nob Hill except to take visiting friends to the Top o' the Mark and is vague about the difference between a cotillion and a pavilion.

Diversity—sociological as well as geographical—is one of the keys to the city's identity. Ever since the Gold Rush attracted men from every continent, San Francisco has had a brilliantly heterogeneous population. There are newspapers published in Chinese, Hungarian, Yugoslav, French, Swedish, Japanese, German, Spanish, Greek, and several other languages, plus half-a-dozen foreign-language radio programs. Scattered throughout the city are about sixty racial and national groups, many of which maintain their own churches, language schools, fraternal organizations, and choral societies.

Garden Court, Sheraton-Palac

Opera House

Fisherman's Wharf

So the San Franciscan may be a bearded Russian Doukhobor ("Spirit Wrestler") living on Potrero Hill, a Mission Street Irishman whose speech still hints of the brogue, or a Frenchman who reads *Le Courrier Français des États-Unis* and attends French language services at Notre Dame des Victoires on Bush Street, founded in 1856. He could be an Icelander who meets with other Scandinavians in October, shortly before the Italians celebrate Columbus Day, to set the record straight as to the "real" discoverer of America—Iceland-born Leif Ericson. He may be a Mexican who lives in the Mission District's Spanish-speaking colony but who still attends Spanish-language Mass at Nuestra Señora de Guadalupe on the Russian Hill slope of North Beach, former site of the Mexican settlement. Similarly, he might be

Longshoremen

a Greek who drives thirty minutes in from the Sunset District to attend Holy Trinity Orthodox Church in the South of Market area, once the center of the Greek colony, meets other Greeks over coffee at the Minerva café on Eddy Street, and donated proudly to the 1955 campaign fund of Mayor George Christopher, first Greek-descended chief executive of a large American city.

The oldest and most tightly knit group of San Franciscans is the city's thirty-five thousand Chinese, most of whom live or work within a few blocks of Grant Avenue between Bush and Broadway. The area is usually described as the largest Chinatown in the world—a claim that may be true if the "world" referred to is the Western world. San Francisco's Chinatown, however, is not merely an Oriental enclave in a Western city but rather a rich and sometimes explosive mixture of cultures—a meeting of East and West that has a picturesque aspect in the shops of Grant Avenue and a less visible but profound impact in the lives of Chinatown's residents.

The meeting of the two worlds is vividly displayed along Sacramento Street, which old-timers call the "Chinese Street," on Grant Avenue, which

Vedanta Temple, Cow Hollow

they still refer to as "Dupont Gai," or along any of the narrow lanes at the eastern foot of Nob Hill. Next door to TV stores are food shops dealing in such commodities as "ancient eggs" and dried octopus. Singsong chants (mostly recorded) drifting out of upper-story windows clash with the rock-'n'-roll rhythms of lunch-counter juke boxes. Old men gather before the offices of the four daily Chinese language papers to read the latest news displayed in the windows, printed in long columns of thousands of characters, each set by hand. In the century-old Taoist Kong Chow Temple on Pine Street off Grant, the altar lamps are simply wicks extending into cans of Wesson oil. Pagoda roofs and brightly colored balconies adorn Chinatown's modern housing project, Ping Yuen. (Because of its hordes of energetic youngsters the project's name has become a standard Chinatown joke; it means "Tranquil Gardens.")

The climactic meeting of old and new comes at Chinese New Year's—extending over a week in late January or February—when Chinese operas and folk dances thousands of years old share the limelight with a much-publicized beauty contest to choose Miss Chinatown, U.S.A. The New Year's parade, witnessed by more occidentals than Chinese, has become San Francisco's biggest annual festival, and the New Year greeting, "Gung hay fat choy!" is used almost as often along Market Street as on Grant Avenue. The procession is dominated by the fierce-headed, block-long Chinese dragon, which serpentines down Grant on the backs of half-a-hundred young men in tennis shoes. The popping of firecrackers, illegal in the city except when

Fisherman's Wharf

*Grant Avenue
at California*

"Chinese Times"

used for "religious purposes," can be heard for miles, set off by enthusiastic youngsters who begin the earsplitting rites weeks in advance and continue long after the New Year is old.

The ways in which East and West meet in Chinatown are not all so obvious, however. Perhaps to an even greater degree than members of the city's other minority groups, the Chinese live in a state of transition between two worlds, a position sometimes rewarding, sometimes painful. The inhabitants of Chinatown face a continual series of decisions as to how to combine the best of the old culture and the new.

A young Chinese-American must decide, for example, whether to follow in his father's footsteps—as a cook or laundryman or Chinatown shopkeeper —or to study for better-paid jobs outside Chinatown, knowing that his opportunities will be limited by his race. When he marries, he and his wife will probably break with ancient custom and establish their own home. One of the notable developments of the past several decades in Chinatown is the breakup of the old family system, in which three generations dwelled under the same roof. Traditionally, the son's mother had absolute authority over his wife, and many a young bride with Western ideas rebelled. So sensitive has this relationship remained today that if the son's mother is widowed she will not move in with his family but with her daughter's.

In everyday living old and new combine in many ways, too. The older woman may wear the traditional black silk trousers around the house (although seldom on the street), but the young wife has probably exchanged hers for the latest in knee-length pants—or for special occasions a Chinese-style sheath with slit skirt. While the family may start the day with corn flakes, they probably end it with a Chinese dinner—provided the wife has had time to shop for the ingredients in several stores along Grant Avenue and to prepare such dishes as steamed pork or beef with Chinese chard. If pressed for time, however, she may settle for meat and potatoes.

Differing traditions of East and West are also represented in Chinatown's religious institutions. About one quarter of Chinatown's families attend such Christian churches as the Holy Family Catholic Mission on Stockton Street or the True Sunshine Episcopal Church on Mason; many others continue the Chinese tradition of private worship within the family, perhaps occasionally

elephone Exchange, Chinatown

visiting one of the Taoist temples such as Tin How, on Waverly Place, or Kong Chow, on Pine. Although there is little place in Chinese tradition for volunteer activities, a Chinese mother in bluejeans may leave her children in Portsmouth Plaza to play while she goes across the street to donate a few hours of labor with hammer and drill in the construction of Buddha's Universal Church.

Education, too, is divided between two traditions. Chinatown children attend late-afternoon Chinese schools as well as the regular public and parochial schools. Grant Avenue at 6 P.M. is clamorous with youngsters just dismissed from their two-hour Chinese-language classes, swinging their satchels and yelling, "You're it!" The children's main interest is usually in regular school activities, however, and most of them drop out of the language classes by the time they reach junior high school.

Because nearly all of Chinatown's residents trace their family origins from areas around Canton, the Chinese spoken along Grant Avenue is mainly Cantonese. Some Mandarin is used, however, mostly by recent refugees from

Young Chinatown at school

China; the Chinese Presbyterian Church, for example, conducts separate services in Mandarin as well as Cantonese and English. As much English as Cantonese is used in Chinatown, and the younger generations mix the language at random. It is common to hear a mother address her child in Chinese and receive her answer in English.

The same mingling of ancient and modern extends into every other phase of life as well. Although there are many well-trained Chinese-American physicians, possibly one third of the residents of Chinatown still have faith in the ancient remedies of herb doctors. Along Grant and Stockton are numerous herb shops, paneled in dark, shiny wood, the walls lined with rows of tiny drawers.

"For surgery, of course I would go to the Chinese Hospital," explained one young Chinatown merchant and civic leader. "But there are some kinds of sickness that Western doctors can't cure. Colds, for example. Herb doctors hold your wrist and tell you what's wrong, and then you have the prescription filled at one of the herb shops. You make tea from the herbs, go to bed, and the next morning you're well!"

Tales of the Chinatown of tong wars, catacombs, and opium dens belong partly to history and partly to fiction. It is still possible to walk down dark alleys off Grant at night and hear from dimly lighted basements the clatter of dominoes in games that could be the illegal *pai gow* but are more probably as legal as poker. Today Chinatown is as free from major crime and delinquency as any part of the city. One reason is the power of Chinatown's organizations over the individual. There is probably no more thoroughly organized community in the nation. It includes dozens of family associations, district organizations, welfare agencies, churches and temples, fraternal and business clubs.

The groups with the tightest hold on the individual are the family associations. In the San Francisco phone book the Joneses are outnumbered by the Lees, a high proportion of them members of one of the largest clans of Chinatown, to which all Chinese Lees belong. Every Lee or Wong or Fong is responsible for every other Lee or Wong or Fong, and although with each new generation the influence of the family decreases, to bring dishonor on the family in any way is still a solemn offense.

Chinatown's top organization is the famed Six Companies, (actually seven), the Chinese Consolidated Benevolent Association, located in a brightly painted yellow, blue, red, and green building on Stockton near Clay, and composed of associations based on the districts around Canton from which San Francisco's Chinese or their forebears originally came. For many decades the organization functioned virtually as a government, so powerful among U. S. Chinese in economic and social matters that any Chinese coming to the U.S. on any mission from China called on the Six Companies first as a matter of protocol. As most Chinese learned English and the community's isolation decreased, the influence of the Six Companies declined until the organization's present functions center on welfare, educational, and social activities.

The tradition of family solidarity not only is a heritage from the rigid society of old China, but was maintained in this country for good reason—self-protection. Thousands of Chinese arrived during the Gold Rush, and in the 1860's thousands more were imported to work on construction of the Central Pacific Railroad. Chinese workers laid the track over the Sierra Nevada and through the deserts to unite the nation by rail at Promontory, Utah. When the railroad was completed, the Oriental workers drifted back to San Francisco, where they joined others newly arrived from China in competing for jobs at near-starvation wages with Caucasian workers. The result was a series of waves of anti-Chinese violence, possibly the worst inflicted on any minority in American history. In self-defense the Chinese withdrew into Chinatown, their own "ghetto." With legitimate means of earning a living cut off, many of them resorted to vice—dope traffic, gambling, prostitution, organized racketeering. In later years, as the anti-Chinese violence subsided, vice declined as well; the law-abiding elders of the community came into control and retained a firm hold.

Chinatown is one of the greatest contradictions in this city of paradoxes. In terms of crowded living quarters and sweatshop working conditions there is little doubt that the area is a near-slum. It is a segregated neighborhood that in some respects still resembles a ghetto. Yet it is also a vivid embodiment of a rich culture, a valuable meeting place of contrasting traditions. Without it the city would scarcely be San Francisco.

Chinese Opera, Chinatown

Chinatown's residents live there partly because of the difficulty of finding housing in other areas, perhaps even more because they admittedly love the place. It gives them a feeling of security rare in modern urban society—a sense of belonging to a well-rooted community in which each is responsible for all. No one anywhere shows more pride in his community than a resident of Chinatown during the annual festivals. With zest and fervor the bands and drum-and-bugle corps blare their theme: "Chinatown, My Chinatown!"

Yet at the same time there is a growing restlessness among members of the rising generation. Many of them want their children to have broader experiences and opportunities than those available in a segregated neighborhood, and move out to the borders of Chinatown and beyond, into such increasingly integrated areas as the inner Richmond. Despite the difficulty of finding housing because of the hostility of many landlords, Chinese-American families live in nearly every neighborhood in the city.

Doubtless the Chinatown of the future will be as different from today's Chinatown as the latter is different from the old Chinatown of queues, tong wars, and opium dens. With the passing of the older generations the residents will increasingly leave their narrow streets and dark alleys and scatter to healthier areas of the city, following the pattern of other minorities who once clustered together in a single neighborhood and are now dispersed—the Irish, the Mexicans, the Greeks.

It is to be hoped, however, that the best of the Chinese heritage will not be lost in the rising tide of standardization and conformity. As Chinatown disappears as a residential neighborhood, it doubtless will remain as a commercial and cultural center. For generations San Franciscans and out-of-town visitors will continue to go to Grant Avenue for the exotic foods, the shops selling teak and jade and Ming trees, the ceremonies and festivals that have made Chinatown one of the brightest facets of this diverse city.

For a vivid experience in the meeting of cultures walk along Broadway near Stockton in the evening; listen to the nasal chant of music from a Chinese movie theater and the lustily sung arias of Verdi and Puccini issuing from the swinging doors of taverns with such names as La Casadoro and Bocce Ball. Although this section is a genuine international settlement, with French, Spanish, Basque, and Mexican cafés and taverns, it is also the meeting ground of Chinatown and North Beach, of Canton and Genoa. North of Broadway on both sides of Columbus Avenue is the city's largest concentration of Italians—a people who are far more fully integrated into the life of the city than the Chinese but who still maintain an active pride in their language, origins, and culture.

Ebullient, responsive, with a generous capacity for the enjoyment of life, the Italian San Franciscan may be a successful lawyer or wine merchant who still sometimes plays the ancient Italian bowling game of bocce ball in the rear of the musical bar of the same name or on the dirt courts at Aquatic Park. He is probably a subscriber to the daily *L'Italia* and a contributor to the fund for setting up the statue of Columbus on Telegraph Hill. He may be a member of the Order of the Sons of Italy, attending the club's regular dinners in Fugazi Hall, which feature ravioli, scallopini, and community singing to the guitar and mandolin. Politics are not likely to be of great importance to him, as one Italian word for politician—*politicante*—has traditionally bad connotations. Such ancestral attitudes have taken a genial

North Beach; Broadway

turn, however, with the Sons of Italy, who cordially endorse all political candidates appearing at their meetings, even though the aspirants may be rivals for the same office.

The North Beach housewife still cooks *alla Italiana* and buys the family *paste* and *vino rosso* along upper Grant or Columbus Avenue. The daughters of the family, at age seven or eight, pose solemnly for the photographer in white confirmation veils and dresses and may later expect big weddings at the Church of Saints Peter and Paul, whose bells will ring out the wedding march over the roof tops of North Beach.

Although some of San Francisco's Italian families date back to the Gold Rush, most of them arrived in the 1880's and '90's at a time when the spread

Produce market

"L'Italia"

of education in Italy meant that Italian immigrants could at last pass the literacy test on Ellis Island. The majority came from Italy's northern provinces—Piedmont, Liguria, Veneto, and Tuscany—and settled in North Beach or on the slopes of Telegraph Hill. Many who had been unskilled laborers or farmers in their homeland were able to shine shoes or work as janitors or scavengers until they saved up enough money to go into business. *Paesani* from the same areas or villages usually went into the same kinds of business and sent for relatives and friends in Italy to come over and help.

From Sicily came many of the fishermen whose two hundred crab boats and forty trawlers dock at Fisherman's Wharf. Such old families as the Aliotos, who operate one of the Wharf's big restaurants, and the Paladinos, who preside over Northern California's largest wholesale fish business, originally from the Sicilian village of Sciacca, where their ancestors for centuries netted fish coming through the narrows of the Mediterranean. Families from Tuscany run the small North Beach stores selling *chianti, pasta,* and *prosciutto.* The wholesale fruit and vegetable concerns crowding San Francisco's produce district are largely owned and operated by immigrants from Genoa.

A son of one Genoese family in the produce business decided that the Italians should have their own banking facilities, rented a building at 1 Columbus Avenue, and opened the Bank of Italy. His name was Amadeo Peter Giannini; his bank, renamed the Bank of America, became the largest in the world; and many residents of North Beach now rank his achievements second only to those of another Genoan, Christopher Columbus.

As they became increasingly prosperous, many North Beach Italians, particularly the second-generation, moved to other neighborhoods in the southeast part of the city or the middle-class Marina; almost as much Italian can be heard along the Marina's Chestnut Street shopping district as along Columbus Avenue itself. But it is an Italian upon which American life has had its impact. Visitors from Italy are sometimes mystified by such a phrase as *"picci in canna"*—a local term for canned peaches.

Many second- and third-generation Italians, however, never use the language except in speaking to the older generation and seldom think of themselves as members of a minority group. They may live in any section of the

Bocce Ball at Aquatic Park

city or its suburbs. Their names are prominent on the society and financial pages and on the membership rolls of the Nob Hill clubs. But most of them still take a vicarious pride in the achievements of a Giannini or a DiMaggio and often correspond with relatives in their ancestral village in Tuscany or Piedmont.

Meanwhile, there are still thousands of first-generation Italians in the city and more continue to arrive, carrying on the cycle. In North Beach old women dressed in black, whose square figures express strength and an ancient people's will to survive, plod along Grant Avenue to market or to mass at St. Francis or Saints Peter and Paul; meeting each other, they pause to talk of children and families in their animated North Beach Italian. Old men whose struggles are finished sit in the sun in Washington Square, listening to the bells of Peter and Paul's toll the hours, discussing the affairs of the world, the baseball scores, the old days in Genoa or Venice. And all generations still turn out en masse for the liveliest of North Beach festivals,

Columbus Day, when a counterpart of the great Genoese lands on the beach at Aquatic Park and parades up Columbus Avenue to receive the acclaim of his transplanted countrymen.

Out in the Western Addition in a small area centering around Post and Buchanan streets, old Victorian houses embellished with exuberant scroll-work display incongruous Oriental-style signs advertising stone lanterns, goldfish, and such dishes as *suki-yaki* and *tempura.* These few blocks are all that remain of "Little Osaka," which before World War II was the home of some six thousand San Franciscans of Japanese ancestry. After spending the war years in relocation camps—or "concentration camps," as the inmates called them—about 80 per cent of the former residents of Little Osaka returned to San Francisco, only to find that the area had been occupied by warworkers—most of them Negroes—who had flooded into the city after Pearl Harbor. Some of the Japanese still owned their homes there and moved back into them as soon as possible. Others scattered to various parts of the city and partly as a result became more integrated into the life of the community than other minorities such as the Chinese.

Over a period of years more of them moved back to Little Osaka, and once again the area has become a commercial and social center of Japanese life, although on a far smaller scale than prewar.

Partly because Japanese immigrants had arrived later and were fewer in number than the Chinese, Little Osaka—even in its heyday—was never a community as thoroughly organized as Chinatown. Its principal organization, the Japanese American Citizens League, contrasts sharply with the traditional Chinatown groupings. The J.A.C.L., whose national headquarters are in San Francisco, has been instrumental in securing for the Japanese Americans the rights taken from them in wartime and in such earlier laws as those forbidding Oriental immigrants to own land or become citizens.

Energetic, thoroughly Americanized, the typical Japanese San Franciscan is likely to have made a successful comeback since the war, particularly if he is a Nisei—member of the second generation. He may be an importer of *kakemono* scrolls and *shoji* screens from Japan, or a wholesale flower merchant specializing in hothouse carnations, gardenias, and chrysanthemums. He may be the proprietor of one of the city's thriving suki-yaki restaurants,

Little Osaka

proud of its popularity among San Franciscans of all races. Through business acumen and an enormous capacity for hard work, he is probably doing even better than he did before the war. On at least one matter most of the Japanese are agreed: the bitter experience of relocation is history and should be forgotten. Books on the subject have been published, but most of the Nisei refuse to read them. "Why get mad all over again?" they ask.

Now dominating the attention of the Nisei is a new-found pride in Japanese culture, aroused by the vogue for Japanese design in architecture, textiles, and ceramics, and by the spate of movies extolling Japanese art and ceremonials. Americans returning from postwar trips to Japan with admiration for the country and its people often asked their Nisei friends questions about the culture, many of which the embarrassed Nisei were unable to answer.

"Before the war," remarked one Nisei, "the emphasis was all on being Americanized. Now we're beginning to wonder if we didn't go too far."

Belatedly the Nisei began to study Japanese art and literature, attend language schools to brush up on the Japanese they had heard at home as children, and swell the audiences for Japanese-made movies formerly attended only by the older generation.

With the rise of the new generation family relationships among the city's Japanese have been sharply altered. Between the Nisei and their immigrant parents, the Issei, there were frequent tensions and misunderstandings. Most of the Issei had arrived in California around the turn of the century, found

International neighborhood on Post Street

English very difficult, and seldom ventured outside the Japanese colony. They often frowned on their children's desire for social activities outside the colony and sometimes forbade them to go dancing with the school crowd or to play football. Most of today's Nisei parents have a very different attitude toward their own children—the third generation, or Sansei. They may want their youngsters to learn the traditional arts of judo or flower-arranging but also encourage them to play in the school band or join the swimming team, hoping for a balance between Americanization and respect for Japanese culture.

Many of the old customs remain or are being revived. The Nisei are as likely to celebrate Girls' Day (March 3) and Boys' Day (May 5) as they are Mothers' or Fathers' Day. New Year's is the time for open house and Oriental foods. Funerals may be the occasion not only for gifts of flowers, Western style, but for the more traditional, and practical, gifts of *koden*—envelopes of money for the bereaved. The churchgoing members of the community are about evenly divided between the Christians and those who worship at one of the five Japanese Buddhist and two Shinto temples.

Some of the traditional ways of life, however, are emphatically rejected by the younger generations. One attractive young Nisei woman who had married a recent immigrant from Japan consented at first to follow the Japanese custom of waiting on her husband in the home. Then the husband received his naturalization papers and became an American citizen. Early the following Sunday morning he woke up his wife and ordered her to get up and fix breakfast as usual. She merely turned over and pulled the blankets up higher.

"You're an American citizen now," she said. "American wives don't have to fix Sunday breakfast. You fix it!"

Before World War II there were only five thousand Negroes in San Francisco. But even prior to Pearl Harbor the population began to expand rapidly. High wartime wages in Bay Area shipyards attracted them by the thousands from the cotton fields and sharecropper cabins of Texas, Arkansas, Mississippi, and Louisiana. Legions of hopeful, dark-skinned people in search of opportunity arrived—like the Joads from the Dust Bowl a few years earlier—in battered old cars piled high with the family's entire possessions. Men, women, and teen-agers were signed up quickly for work around the ship-yards; some learned to weld, rivet, drive trucks, and operate machinery.

Housing was a major problem. Wherever in the Bay Area a handful of Negroes had been living, several times as many newcomers moved into the neighborhood. Traditionally, most of San Francisco's Negroes had lived in an area of a few blocks just west of Fillmore between Geary and Pine—in

Three artists

the city's oldest dwellings, the once-fashionable gingerbread houses of the Western Addition. The influx continued until the decrepit old dwellings—many of them holding several families each—were jammed to the bursting point. Smaller Negro neighborhoods grew up in the vicinity of Hunters Point. Altogether there are now more than fifty thousand Negroes in the city, ten times as many as prewar.

When the wartime shipyard boom collapsed, many a Negro family found itself living on unemployment compensation. In other West Coast areas Negroes could be gradually absorbed into the growing postwar industries, but San Francisco, largely a non-industrial, white-collar city, offered few opportunities for people with little education or training. As a result there were several applicants for every opening in the traditional Negro jobs—janitors, domestics, culinary workers. Negroes from Northern cities who could qualify for well-paid jobs on a skilled level found employers often unwilling to hire them—even in this traditionally tolerant city. Although the job situation eased somewhat in the following years, unemployment is perennially high in the Fillmore District.

"A Negro can get anything in San Francisco," they say in the Fillmore. "He can get a room in the best hotels. He can get a meal at the best restaurants. He can get called 'Mister.' He can get anything—except a job."

There are additional reasons for bitterness. Finding housing outside the congested Fillmore area is extremely difficult for all but higher-income groups. The Fillmore is not only a slum but a largely white-owned slum, which causes Negroes to feel, with some justification, that whites are profiting from the conditions under which whites force them to live. Several government housing projects provide better living conditions for low-income families but can accommodate only a small fraction of the total demand. Although most of the Fillmore had been officially condemned as a blighted area, redevelopment of the district has been chronically retarded by the difficulty of finding non-discriminatory low-cost housing into which the present residents of the area can move.

Restricted in jobs and housing, the Negro often reacts with intensified suspicions and sensitivities. In extreme cases such frustration leads to desperation and violence. With only 7 per cent of the city's population, Negroes commit from 20 per cent to 40 per cent of the crimes, particularly robberies and assaults—part of the price the city pays for racial discrimination.

But there are elements of hope in the situation. Even though San Francisco is a white-collar city, it is also a port city, with thousands of jobs on the docks. Fortunately the International Longshoremen's and Warehousemen's Union, which controls employment on the waterfront, has long been free of

Pete's Market

color barriers, and Negroes who in wartime had helped build the ships of the nation's merchant marine found jobs loading and unloading the same ships along the Embarcadero. The Municipal Railway is another area of opportunity open to all races, and there are Negro drivers on many of the city's busses, streetcars, and cable cars. San Francisco in 1957 was the first city in California to set up a fair-employment commission, opening up other occupations, and Negroes began to appear for the first time as cab and truck drivers and in other capacities.

With sufficient income it is possible for Negroes to find good housing. Those who are willing to face the humiliation of being told repeatedly, "You can't live here," may eventually find homes in predominantly white areas, and there is a scattering of Negro families in most of the city's neighborhoods. There are also highly desirable neighborhoods with mixed racial populations, such as Merced Heights and Ingleside Terrace, which command sweeping views of the southwestern part of the city, the coast line, and the ocean.

But the center of Negro life in San Francisco continues to be Fillmore Street, which despite its tawdry aspects is full of verve and spirit—brilliant flashing signs, jazzed-up store fronts, blaring juke boxes. Fillmore's night-time crowds are larger than those of any other neighborhood in the city. Many Fillmore residents love the pageantry and liveliness of nighttime city life, which contrasts sharply with the rural areas from which most of them came. They are also fond of the foods they ate in the South—rice, grits, sweet-potato pie, "hog maul and chitlin's."

Perhaps the most important part of the Southern heritage is the attachment to the churches—the only form of Negro organization in many parts of the South and the principal center of social life. Such Fillmore District churches as the Glad Tidings Temple, the New Strangers Home Baptist Church, and the Greater Liveoak Baptist Church carry on the tradition.

There are several large major-denominational churches in the Fillmore, but newcomers often feel lost in the big organizations, and a dozen or more members may split off to form their own church on a more intimate basis—in the Southern pattern.

The larger churches are important for another reason as well. Their memberships tend to cut across class lines, and they are the only organizations in the Fillmore that even begin to bridge the gulf dividing the Negro community between the educated and the uneducated. Outside the churches the two groups find little in common socially, and the educated Negro—who is likely, in San Francisco, to have friends and associates among whites—is frequently regarded with suspicion by the colored emigrants from the South. Attempts to bridge the gulf are made by the two Negro weekly newspapers, the *Sun-Reporter* and the *Independent,* and by such action groups as the Urban League and the National Association for the Advancement of Colored People. But with few exceptions there is a lack of leadership that can unite both elements of the community as a civic or political force. The intellectual Negroes who make the attempt encounter obstacles that sometimes seem insuperable; they must cope with another legacy of the South—the Southern Negro's image of himself as a second-class citizen without rights or privileges or the power to improve his own condition.

Yet there is a ferment in the air around Fillmore Street that can be sensed by even the most uneducated. The old feeling of hopelessness is slowly passing. The intense interest in Southern desegregation and the enactment of San Francisco and California fair-employment legislation are signs of the times. The achievements of individual Negroes in the arts and professions and in civic affairs inspire others to try to break the barriers. One Fillmore leader expressed the feelings of many of his people in commenting on the fact that one Negro had become a San Francisco municipal judge and another an assistant district attorney.

"We don't want an assistant district attorney!" he insisted, thumping the table. "We want a district attorney!"

At the opposite end of the social and economic scale from San Francisco's Negro colony is its Jewish community. The fifty-five thousand Jewish San

Franciscans are so thoroughly integrated into the city that it is only in a limited sense that they can be referred to as a community at all.

Significantly, there is no single area of the city that can be considered a Jewish neighborhood. Jews live everywhere from the curved streets of the Marina and the mansions of Pacific Heights to the steep slopes of Visitacion Valley. They provide leadership for all kinds of civic groups from the United Crusade to the Chamber of Commerce. They serve as supervisors, judges, members of many city commissions, and leaders of both political parties. Unlike members of any of the city's other minorities, except the Italians, many Jews can fit the picture of the traditional socialite "Mr. San Francisco" of the society and gossip columns.

The fortunate position of the Jew in San Francisco began with the Forty-Niners. German and French Jews celebrated the High Holy Days of 1849 in a tent on the waterfront, and some went into business as merchants and money brokers. Some of the institutions they established developed eventually into the large department stores and banks that helped make the city the commercial center of the West—the London-Paris National Bank, for example (now merged with Crocker-Anglo). Such Jewish families as the Fleishhackers (banking), the Zellerbachs (paper products), the Strausses, Sterns, and Haases ("levi's," whose riveted pockets were invented by Levi Strauss a century ago to hold miners' nuggets) span most of the history of the city and continue to provide civic leadership. San Francisco's Jews are the wealthiest per capita in the country and have provided strong financial support for the city's symphony, opera, and museums. Jewish philanthropists have been responsible for the creation of such San Francisco landmarks as Fleishhacker Zoo and Pool, Stern Grove, Steinhart Aquarium, and Sutro Heights.

Oddly, the only significant cleavage in the Jewish community arises in part from the fortunate position Jews occupy in San Francisco. At times there have been sharp differences of opinion over the extent to which the traditions of Judaism should be preserved. The situation is the reverse of that existing among most other minorities; it is the members of the younger generation who have sometimes censured the elders for neglecting the common tradition.

Temple Emanu-El

The older Jewish leaders, scions of families that had been pillars of the community for generations, felt little in common with the old militant Judaism bred in the ghettos of Europe. The formative years of the younger generation, however, came during the era of the nazi concentration camps and the fight for the independence and integrity of Israel. The younger Jews felt that their elders were neglecting Judaism to the point of endangering the sense of identity basic to Jewish life. The controversy reached a high point in the years immediately after World War II but later diminished, partly as a result of the pride of all Jews in the achievements of Israel, partly as a consequence of the contemporary American emphasis on churchgoing, which has affected Jews as well as Christians.

In San Francisco's Jewish community the result has been to swell the rolls of the conservative synagogues and crowd classrooms with children studying Jewish history. Youngsters coming home from Sunday school have surprised their non-religious parents with requests to light the candles on Friday evening in accordance with ancient ritual.

"Times have changed," a Jewish leader commented. "A generation ago Jewish parents had to explain to their children what a Jew was. Now," he smiled, "they have to explain what a non-Jew is.

"Then, too, parents used to reassure their children that Jews were as good as non-Jews. Now they have to explain that non-Jews are as good as Jews."

San Francisco's Jews are not the only group that has confronted the problem of being drawn toward opposite poles; this is a conflict that faces all of the city's minorities in various forms. Pulling in one direction is the desire to drop the group identity as clannish and obsolete and to integrate completely with the majority. Pulling in the other is the sense of rootedness in a tradition and a need to preserve its values, a pull intensified, perhaps, during an era in which all Americans are more group-conscious than ever.

The result is a set of conflicts: among the Chinese the conflict between loyalty to Chinatown and the desire to move out; among the Japanese between the revival of the national culture and the wish to be as Americanized as possible. Even among the younger-generation Italians, long "integrated" into the city, there is a nostalgia for the old customs evident in the planned revival of such festivities as the Mardi Gras Carnevale. Among the Negroes—clearly the most underprivileged group—the pull is overwhelmingly stronger in one direction; although some Negro leaders try to stress Negro history and tradition, by and large there is a far greater emphasis on the desire for integration and the achievement of basic human rights. The day seems far distant when the Negro will be in a position to ask the question the Nisei have posed in regard to integration: "Have we gone too far?"

Meanwhile there are more urgent questions for all San Franciscans. How well does San Francisco allow members of its minorities to make the choices

A local institution,
the Guckenheimer Sauerkraut Band,
moves on

between tradition and integration, to work out their own destinies freely without harassment and discrimination? How well does San Francisco deserve its reputation as a racially tolerant, cosmopolitan city, encouraging differences and emphasizing diversity?

There is considerable evidence that the reputation is not entirely justified. Although racial and religious discrimination may be less flagrant in San Francisco than elsewhere, it exists at least covertly at many levels. Even the Jews find certain doors closed, or open only on a quota basis, primarily among the top-ranking private clubs. Although most San Francisco firms do not discriminate against Jewish job applicants, the local offices of some national corporations often do so—unofficially.

Orientals frequently find employment opportunities limited in white-

San Francisco State College

collar and public-contact work, although to a lesser extent than Negroes do. Even in non-white-collar work the Negro will sometimes find that not only employers but white unions will not accept him. And Orientals as well as Negroes encounter unwritten housing restrictions. Although San Franciscans of all races are usually admitted without question to the first-class hotels and restaurants, there are unofficial color barriers in some of the lower-priced hotels, which many minority-group members are more likely to be able to afford.

On the other hand, these restrictions must be balanced against contrary evidence. Many of the job barriers are breaking down. During World War II Chinese girls began to be hired as secretaries in the financial district, and within the following decade the practice of having Oriental employees in an office or a store came to be commonplace. In a few offices and plants the custom is beginning to include Negroes as well, and there are indications that the practice will spread. The construction industry is beginning to welcome qualified Negroes, and many of the city's hospitals hire staff employees

Shoppers cross Stockton Stree

on merit without regard to race. Fair-employment legislation can be expected slowly to continue opening other job areas.

Similar break-throughs are being made in the field of housing. Despite difficulties non-whites continue to find homes in previously unmixed neighborhoods. When the new families move in, they are likely to find the neighbors friendlier than would be the case in most other U.S. cities. In both jobs and housing many of the expanded opportunities for minorities have been created through diligent effort by the city's strong Council for Civic Unity, a citizens' organization with membership including top leaders of business, labor, and the professions.

As important as the specific job and housing opportunities is the general atmosphere of San Francisco. In a city proud of its cosmopolitan tradition, racial and religious prejudice is unfashionable, and bigots find it advisable

to keep their opinions to themselves. Increasingly, service clubs include non-Caucasians; several local chapters of a major service club indignantly withdrew from their national organization rather than follow orders to expel their Oriental members. Negroes, Caucasians, and Orientals form foursomes on the city's public tennis courts, play together in professional jazz bands or amateur orchestras organized in the playgrounds, argue together over the coffee tables of North Beach, sing together in the Bach Choir, and worship together in a number of the city's churches. Of the last-mentioned, the unique Church for the Fellowship of All Peoples—a highly successful experiment in religious integration—is a distinguished example of the ways in which San Franciscans are breaking new ground in human relations. Its non-denominational Protestant services and its imaginative intercultural program enable people of varied races and creeds to find in the experience of common worship an affirmation of their deepest convictions and values.

Despite oppressive restrictions that remain it is probable that San Francisco opens more doors to people of all races and backgrounds than any other city in the nation. Many doors remain to be opened. But the basic requirement for opening them is present—a growing recognition that the city's rich racial and cultural diversity is as vital an element of San Francisco's unique character as the diversity of its landscape.

Fellowship Church

648
F. CITRARO
BAIL BONDS
A. BOYD
PUCCINELLI
700
AABAIL
KEN TILLES
BAIL BONDS
Coca-Cola
COCKTAILS
SANDWICHES
BAIL BAIL
TELEPHONE

Near Ferry Building

Fisherman's Wharf

Kearny Street near old Hall of Justice

Rain on
Montgomery Street

Skyline and Bay Bridge

Fog over Twin Peaks

Appraisers Building (Federal)

CHAPTER V

Centers of Power

They begin arriving before eight o'clock every weekday morning, first by the hundreds, then by the thousands.

They converge on San Francisco by the carload, the busload, the trainload, coming across the Bay Bridge, up the Peninsula, down from Marin, to the East Bay Terminal, the Southern Pacific depot, the Ferry Building, and downtown parking lots and garages. Joined by other thousands from the outlying areas of the city, they head for a small area of about a dozen square blocks centering around Montgomery and Bush streets.

They flow into giant hives of steel and concrete ten and twenty and thirty stories high. Eight hours later they pour into the streets again and out of the city, and by six o'clock the great hives are empty.

This area of half a square mile is the economic heart of San Francisco, of Northern California, and in some respects of the entire West. The ebb and flow of its legions of workers are the daily systole and diastole pumping the lifeblood of the Western economy. Here are expended incalculable amounts of human energy. Each cell of this complex structure encompasses unmeasured toil and sweat and tears, as well as ulcers, aches, and hypertension.

Yet this vast expenditure of energy by an army of workers produces almost nothing tangible. Out of the Montgomery Street area come no usable commodities, no steaks or shoes or houses or automobiles or television sets. Its main products are decisions. Its principal technique is guesswork. Holding the commanding positions in this army, housed in the upper levels of Montgomery Street with views of the city and bay, are the Chief Guessers. They must guess what the masses of people want—or can be induced to want. They must predict within very narrow margins of error how much oil or paper or electricity or insurance or canned fruit the people of the West need or can be persuaded to buy. And they must guess which of all possible means of production and persuasion and distribution will enable their companies to pay expenses and make a profit. Or they must be able to choose lieutenants who can make these guesses for them, and choosing Lieutenant Guessers is the most risky guesswork of all.

San Francisco Stock Exchange

Montgomery Street

All of these guesses must be educated guesses, if the wheels are to be kept turning. And so the Chief Guessers and Lieutenant Guessers assemble about them battalions of experts, from engineers to advertisers, who can supply the necessary education, and battalions of communicators, from typists to telecom operators, who can maintain contact with their factories, railroads, ships, refineries, branches, substations, farms, stores, and warehouses. These are the multitudes of Montgomery Street, and their main duty is to enable the Chief Guessers, the Lieutenant Guessers, and the Buck Private Guessers to make more accurate guesses.

But the function of Montgomery Street is more than guessing. The guesses themselves are the basis for decisions; the guessers are also deciders; the experts are also expediters. To make a decision is to exert power. And the skyscrapers of Montgomery Street are centers of power. From the top floors of the downtown buildings of San Francisco lines of power reach out to all parts of the state and the West—power to provide money and communications and transportation and electric energy, power to mobilize the resources of mines and oil fields, forests and farmlands, and to direct the labor of millions of employees in ways that are socially wise or foolish. The towers of Montgomery Street are the colossi of the Western economy.

The undisputed number-one colossus of Montgomery Street is the booming giant of the West, the largest non-government banking institution in the world, the Bank of America. Its head office at Montgomery and California is a prime example of Emerson's dictum that an institution is the lengthened shadow of one man. The long shadow that falls across the big building at California and Montgomery—and across smaller buildings in several hundred California towns and cities—is that of one of the two or three financial wizards America has produced, A. P. Giannini.

"A.P." was that contradiction in terms, a revolutionary banker. Every modern American bank has felt the repercussions of his revolution and has adopted some of his principles.

After the earthquake and fire of 1906 Giannini's young bank was the first to be reopened in the smoldering city. He set up some planks and barrels on the waterfront and went into business with funds he had hauled out of the

Downtown

burning area in a wagon. Over the years to come he built his institution on the basis of a single revolutionary principle—to "bring the bank to the people." His purpose was to serve not only the big investors and borrowers, who had been the chief patrons of banks up to that time, but millions of people who had never before used a bank, who had a few dollars to save or wanted a few to borrow. Among Giannini's innovations were small personal loans and statewide branch banking, which enables a community to avail itself of a credit system not dependent on the ups and downs of the local economy. Statewide banking balances the economy of one part of the state against the others and has been a major factor in the unprecedented economic growth of California. There is a branch of Giannini's bank at nearly every town, village, and crossroads in the state, and it is well known that the thirsty prospector stumbling across the sands of California's deserts will have more trouble finding water than getting a loan from the Bank of America's nearest branch.

The brain center of this financial empire is on the eleventh floor of the Montgomery Street head office. Extending the entire length of the building are the offices of the top executives. The arrangement is similar to that of most other executive floors with one exception—these offices have no walls. Giannini insisted that the officers of the branch banks should not be hidden away in private cloisters—an old banking tradition—but should do business out in the open, always visible and available to the public, and the same practice is followed all the way from the smallest branch up to the Montgomery Street headquarters. From his desk in one corner of the eleventh floor A.P. was in a position to bellow instructions to any of his lieutenants— and frequently did. Although A.P. died in 1949, his presence is still felt in the big room. In this office are made the decisions on general bank policy affecting the bank's seven million accounts, its more than ten billion dollars in deposits, and its branches and representatives in sixteen foreign countries.

San Francisco's reputation as a banking center does not rest solely with the Bank of America. On Sansome Street is the third-largest of the nation's Federal Reserve Banks. Another four of the nation's fifty biggest commercial banks are headquartered here: American Trust and Wells-Fargo (which merged in 1960), and Crocker-Anglo are the two largest, followed by the

Market Street

fast-growing new First Western Bank, founded by former associates of Giannini who aspire to set up a statewide system similar to the Bank of America; and the Bank of California, housed in an awe-inspiring Greek temple at California and Sansome.

The Big Four of San Francisco's non-banking colossi rear their imperial towers within a few blocks of each other: Pacific Telephone and Telegraph, Standard Oil of California, Southern Pacific, and Pacific Gas and Electric.

In a large office on the eighteenth floor of the Telephone Building at New Montgomery near Mission (the building designed by Timothy Pfleuger) sits the man responsible for the thousands of miles of communication wire that keep the economy of the West running—the president of Pacific Telephone. To keep up with the explosive population growth of the region, he has to be responsible for the installation of one new telephone somewhere in the West at the rate of one every ninety seconds every hour of every day in the year. Along with the new phones must be provided new wires and trunk lines, new personnel to install them, new switchboards and operators and repair trucks and central offices, new engineers, accountants, linemen, cable splicers, and operators of snow cats and helicopters to service remote installations in mountains and deserts.

Mechanics' Monument; to right: SP, Matson, PG & E

California Street; up Nob Hill

This man on the eighteenth floor of the Telephone Building heads an organization that must be prepared to meet a continual series of emergencies. Despite all precautions his thousands of miles of wire are vulnerable to the vicissitudes of wind, weather, and human error—to boring insects and tunneling rodents, to the processes of corrosion and freezing, to low-flying airplanes, the deep-cutting plows of farmers, the steam shovels of excavators, and the errant anchors of ships.

When a break occurs in a single circuit, possibly interrupting hundreds of phone calls, the circuit must be immediately rerouted over other wires. Battalions of engineers work out schedules to anticipate every conceivable interruption. The schedules are filed at the Traffic Control Center on the second floor of the Telephone Building. There a long semicircular board similar to those in stock exchanges records the location of each break in the lines and the present current loads on all other lines. By observing the board the specialists in the room can learn which circuits are available for handling additional calls and which are filled to capacity at any given moment. Within seconds they reroute the calls over available circuits possibly hundreds of miles away.

The separate telephone exchanges for the city of San Francisco are located in a dozen buildings throughout the city, staffed by several thousand operators and other workers. But the twenty-six-story tower on New Montgomery Street is the home office of more than eighty thousand employees and the nerve center of communications for five Western states.

As vital to the economy as the wires that keep it in communication is the petroleum that keeps the engines running. The focal point of the West's largest petroleum network is the twenty-two-story Italian Renaissance headquarters of the Standard Oil Company of California just off Montgomery on Bush. From the executive suite on the eighteenth floor is governed an enterprise that pumps or refines or explores for oil in twenty countries on every continent of the earth—except Antarctica, which may yet be added to the list. The men on that floor must make the decisions that keep petroleum flowing from thousands of wells through hundreds of miles of pipe lines to tank cars and tank ships that transport it to the West's largest refineries (one of them is across the bay at Richmond) at the rate of a million gallons every hour, day, and night the year round.

On the eighteenth floor of the Bush Street building was made a series of decisions that had a profound effect on the international balance of power. As early as the 1920's, Standard's executives on Bush Street, studying innumerable charts, diagrams, statistics, and field reports, faced an ominous fact: the supply of crude oil underground in California—and in the entire U.S.—was limited, but the growth potential of the Western economy was unlimited. Sooner or later they would have to import oil on a large scale if the wheels of the economy—and of Standard's refineries—were to be kept running.

Quietly they began to send out teams of explorers, geologists, and drillers to probe the crust of the earth. In 1932 the drillers struck a productive field in an unlikely spot—the island of Bahrein off the coast of Arabia. But their island strike, like the landing of Columbus at San Salvador, seemed to presage greater discoveries.

The men on Bush Street weighed the odds and decided to take the gamble. In 1933 they negotiated a pact with King Ibn Saud for oil rights in the sterile sands of Saudi Arabia, and combined with other oil companies to form the Arabian-American Oil Company—Aramco. But after two years of drilling in the blistering heat Aramco found little more than a few oily puddles— not enough to bother hauling to the coast, six miles away. The men in the executive offices at Standard had to make some agonizing decisions. Could they afford to sink more millions in the Arabian sands on the chance that oil might lie deeper? Seldom have any of the Chief Guessers of Montgomery Street made more hazardous guesses. In the end they sent out the word to keep drilling.

In March of 1938 a wildcat well probing 4700 feet beneath the desert suddenly hit the jackpot. It tapped the greatest oil reserves yet discovered on earth. At that moment, for better or for worse, the United States became a power in the Middle East.

Saudi Arabia is now one of the major sources of oil for the free world. Its production at present is far in excess of U.S. needs, and most of its oil is sold in Europe. But the men on Bush Street, aware of the shifting political sands of the Middle East, continue to send out explorers to other parts of the world. As a result they now have large producing fields not only all over the United States but in Venezuela and Sumatra, the latter supplying about a quarter of the crude oil flowing into Standard's California refineries. Only a small proportion of the products coming out of the refineries is sold in service stations. The rest are chemicals that go into the production of plastics, Dacron clothing, paints, soap and detergents, plywood, fertilizer, and a hundred or so other products.

The men in the massive, high-columned building on Bush Street thus govern a corporation that produces 28 per cent of the petroleum products consumed in the West, is one of the seven great international oil companies, and by several measures is one of the dozen giants of American industry.

Three blocks from the Standard Building, at the eastern edge of the financial district where California meets Market, is a ten-story building topped by an electric sign that with its pedestal is nearly half the height of the building itself. Looming high on the downtown horizon, it consists of two thirty-five-foot letters: "SP."

Old-timers in the city wince at the sign and profess to see symbolism in its domination of the skyline. Actually it was erected about sixty years too late to be symbolic. Around the turn of the century it would have been symbolic indeed. For three decades, from 1880 to 1910, the Southern Pacific Railroad (originally Central Pacific), founded by the railroad titans, Huntington, Stanford, Crocker, and Hopkins, was the sole colossus bestriding all of California, dominating the economic and political life of the state. In 1910 the railroad's political machine was defeated by a reform movement headed by Hiram Johnson, elected governor on an anti-SP ticket. Since then the railroad has sedulously avoided throwing its weight around, and the era when it was known as the "octopus" is long-gone history.

But SP is still quite a colossus; it is one of the nation's three largest railroads (the others are the Pennsylvania and New York Central). The executives under the big sign on the building at California and Market, however, are less concerned with their ranking among railroads than with devising ways to meet the continual challenge of competition from other forms of

California Street; down Nob Hill

transportation. Their strategy has been to meet the competitor on his own grounds and go him one better. They have responded to the challenge of the trucking lines by acquiring truck fleets of their own (which now operate over more mileage than do their trains), combining the advantages of the two forms of transportation by putting the trucks on the train, "piggyback" style, and providing shippers with doorstep delivery.

They have built more than a thousand miles of pipe lines to transport petroleum more efficiently than it can be carried either by tank cars or tank trucks. They have further diversified the railroad's operation by adding to the company's widespread holdings of income property, timber lands, farms, mines, cattle ranches, and particularly land for industrial purposes. With four million acres of such property (and income from another million and a half) SP is one of the largest landholders in the nation. But the backbone of SP is still its rail system, and the men on Market Street are chiefly concerned with hauling freight and people in 90,000 cars on 20,000 miles of rails extending over an area from Portland, Oregon, to New Orleans—a region they call the Golden Empire.

Busses and planes carry so many people these days that for the railroad passengers are now a minor side line, accounting for only 5 per cent of the company's income. And four fifths of all the railroad's passenger miles are racked up by the commuters who are hauled up the Peninsula to San Francisco every morning and back at night. Far more important to the railroad are its heavy cargoes of rock and ore, steel, lumber, gasoline, packaged foods, cotton, sugar beets. For carrying these bulky cargoes, the rails are still supreme. But the men at California and Market are looking beyond SP's rails—beyond even its trucks and lands and pipe lines. They have high hopes for legislative changes which would enable them to add to their vast transportation system not only busses but boats and planes as well.

SP is the oldest of San Francisco's economic colossi, but no grass is visible between its rails. The Golden Empire is on the move.

At Market and Beale, one block from the SP building, in the seventeen-story classic granite edifice designed by Arthur Brown, Jr., is the head office of the organization that in terms of plant and area is the largest private power utility in the nation—the Pacific Gas and Electric Company.

The PG & E occupies the most crucial position of any of the city's business giants. Knock out PG & E and the wheels would stop turning immediately all over Northern and Central California. The lights would go out; the elevators would stop running; no meals would be cooked; no water would be pumped.

The man in the presidential suite on the fourteenth floor of the PG & E Market Street headquarters shoulders an awesome responsibility. He must keep the gas moving through 20,000 miles of pipe lines and the electricity flowing over 70,000 miles of power conduits over an area roughly the size of Great Britain.

The fuel that cooks the meals in San Francisco makes a long trip before it even reaches the 20,000-mile network that distributes it to the kitchen stoves. It comes through two thirty-inch pipe lines snaking across deserts and mountains from the gas fields in Texas more than 1600 miles away. This great distance from the source creates monumental problems for the men at Market and Beale. The gas must be kept flowing through the pipe line at a fairly steady rate; it cannot fall below a certain minimum or rise above a specific maximum. But the amount of gas used by consumers goes through wild fluctuations from hour to hour, day to day, and season to season. The greatest peaks in demand are caused by cold weather, when millions of stoves and furnaces are turned on. For every one-degree drop in the temperature below sixty-five, the men on Market Street must supply an additional 42,000,000 cubic feet of gas every twenty-four hours.

One way to meet the peaks of demand is to draw on such gas holders as the big $5,000,000 tank in San Francisco's Potrero district. But the gas holders do not store nearly enough for the area's growing needs, and PG & E employees are forced continually to devise ways of storing the fuel elsewhere—such as in natural subterranean reservoirs in the Central Valley that once held gas but have been nearly emptied by use.

Another way to help meet the additional demand is simply to phone the gas suppliers in Texas and ask them to increase the amount coming through the pipe lines. It takes two days, however, for the added gas pressure to flow through the 1600-mile conduits, and when people want extra gas in cold weather they want it now—not two days later. On the twelfth floor of the Market Street building is a completely equipped weather department with a dozen meteorologists whose job is to predict how far the temperature is going to rise or fall several days in advance at all points over the entire territory. From their predictions the gas department must try to calculate how much of the fuel to order from Texas to keep the customers warm next week in San Francisco and all over Northern California.

The men in the Electric Operations Department in the big gray building at Market and Beale have similar problems. The electricity is generated in two kinds of plants, steam and hydro. Most of PG & E's electricity—about 75 per cent—comes from fourteen big plants with dynamos turned by steam power. Half the steam plants are around San Francisco Bay. Two are in the city itself, at Potrero and Hunters Point, and the largest private steam plant in the West is on the shore of the northern arm of the bay near Pittsburg.

The other 25 per cent of PG & E's power comes, via a network of power lines blanketing most of the state, from sixty-two hydroelectric plants with dynamos turned by the falling water of California's rivers, most of them in the Sierra Nevada. A tiny fraction of the power fed into the PG & E grid comes from the energy of the splitting atom. The reactor at Vallecitos, east of San Francisco Bay near Livermore, constructed jointly by PG & E and General Electric, was the first privately financed nuclear plant in the world. The reactor produces heat to make the steam that spins the turbine generators that produce the electricity. A much larger nuclear plant is under construction at Eureka, three hundred miles north of San Francisco, and an entirely new kind of plant is being built near Geyserville to make use of the steam that spurts naturally from vents in the earth's crust, the first geothermal steam plant in the U.S.

The problem of fluctuations in demand is even more worrisome to the men at PG & E in the electric department than those in the gas department. No receptacles have as yet been devised that will store electricity as a tank stores gas. It has to be made to order, requiring great reserve capacities to meet all possible demand. The demand for power, like that for gas, zooms up at breakfast time, reaches various peaks during the day and tapers off at bedtime when the television tubes quit burning. In December millions of Christmas-tree lights require a big step-up in the output, but even that peak is exceeded in the summertime when California's farmers switch on thousands of pumps to irrigate their crops.

The size and timing of the peak loads thus depend—among other things— on the weather, the rainfall, and the runoff from the Sierra snow pack. The superintendent of power control in the classic granite building on Market Street has to be responsible for continual calculations to determine which of his seventy-five hydro and steam plants all over the state are capable of carrying at any particular moment additional loads—and in what proportions—to cope with every conceivable contingency including inevitable plant shutdowns and line interruptions at various points over PG & E's 70,000 miles of wire. None of the Chief Guessers of Montgomery Street has a tougher job.

Standing shoulder to shoulder with PG & E on Market Street is a colossus of ships, the cupola-topped capital of the Matson Navigation Company. As

Matson dock

Chicago was built by railroads, so San Francisco was built by ships, and the ten miles of piers along the shore of the bay are in one sense the economic spinal cord of the city. Captain William Matson in the 1880's founded the oldest of the city's home-owned big-three shipping lines when he began to haul sugar cane from Hawaii to the mainland. The fleet of vessels with the big "M" on the funnels constitutes the economic life line of the Hawaiian economy. Captain Matson's successors in the Market Street building have a particular interest in a highly profitable cargo whose tonnage has sky-rocketed in recent years—tourists. Most of the Matson's vacationers sail to Honolulu on two big white Matson liners, the *Lurline* and the *Matsonia*, but increasing numbers board the *Mariposa* and *Monterey* for trips to Australia and the South Pacific.

Aside from the Matson Building, San Francisco's shipping row is concentrated along lower California Street two or three blocks away. Here are the offices of the marine insurance companies, the agents of world steamship lines, and one building that, like the Matson headquarters, still reflects the personality of one man. Captain Robert Dollar, a shrewd old Scot with a touch of genius who occupied the corner office on the tenth floor of the structure bearing his name, headed America's largest shipping empire—the Dollar Lines—and was still launching transpacific luxury liners during the Depression just before his death at age eighty-eight. Renamed the American President Lines, the company sends three-dozen ships around the globe over 90,000 miles of sea routes. Its fleet of luxury liners, led by the flagship *President Cleveland* and its sister ship, the *President Wilson,* has proved insufficient to handle the growing passenger traffic to the Orient, and APL has on the drawing boards a 43,000-ton superliner for the transpacific run. The Dollar Building has proved too small to handle the expanding company itself, which is scheduled to move into a striking new twenty-one-story tower at Kearny and California.

Also quartered in the Dollar Building is the third and newest of the city's three big shipping companies, Pacific Far East Lines, founded by former protégés of Captain Dollar to supplement and compete with APL in the growing Orient trade.

Produce market

Embarcadero

South of Ferry Building; Bay Bridge

Besides the major national corporations with regional headquarters here (in such lines as steel, electric equipment, railroads, and air lines) San Francisco is the home office of several other locally owned industrial giants. The spectacular twenty-story slab of green glass at Market and Battery is headquarters of the Crown-Zellerbach Corporation, which began in 1870 as a stationery store opened by Anthony Zellerbach in a basement at Commercial and Sansome and became the nation's second-largest paper manufacturer. Near the Bay Bridge terminal is the brain center of California Packing Corporation, the world's largest canner of fruit and vegetables, most of them from the rich alluvial soil of California's four-hundred-mile-long Central Valley.

Not all of the city's centers of power are business concerns. San Francisco has traditionally been a stronghold of organized labor and a high-wage area, with the maritime unions occupying key positions. The biggest are the Sailors Union of the Pacific, with headquarters on Harrison near the First Street entrance to the Bay Bridge, and the International Longshoremen's and Warehousemen's Union on Golden Gate near Market; ILWU's local occupies a startling new hexagonal building near Fisherman's Wharf.

North from Telegraph Hill

Exceptions to the rule that nothing tangible is manufactured in San Francisco are the printing plants, most of which are located behind the Embarcadero (and which turn out, among other products, labels and advertising material), and the aromatic coffee roasters near the Bay Bridge, which refine one twelfth of all the world's coffee.

Particularly significant in terms of this area's future are the great engineering firms, Morrison-Knudson International in the Equitable Building, Utah Construction in the Shell Building, Bechtel International a block up Bush in the Mills Building, and Kaiser Engineers across the bay in Oakland. Having built the mammoth engineering projects of the West—Hoover Dam, Grand Coulee, Central Valley—these "earth changers" are now constructing dams, roads, factories, and power plants around the world. Together with the city's maritime and industrial leaders, they are looking west beyond the Golden

Gate to the immeasurable opportunities offered by the industrialization of the undeveloped regions in Asia, Africa, and Latin America.

For a century San Francisco has been the magnet and nerve center of the burgeoning West; and the towers of Montgomery Street—with their legions of Guessers, Deciders, Experts, Communicators, and Expediters operating the Western economy—now seem destined to become one of the nerve centers of the new westward movement of capital and skills and men to the awakening lands around the Pacific.

Night skyline from the south

North Beach; Columbus Avenue

Powell Street; afternoo

Richardson
Bay

Muir Woods

Sausalito, smelt fishermen

Fort Cronkhite

Raccoon Strait

El Cerrito, Richmond, Mount Tamalpais

Aladema Naval Air Station

Woodside

Near Half Moon Bay

Elementary School, Westlake

Lookout near Point Lobos

Sausalito

Corinthian Island

Near Marina Yacht Harbor

Sausalito from Belvedere

Lincoln Park

CHAPTER VI

Breathing Spaces

Frederick Law Omsted, Sr., the eminent conservationist and designer of New York's Central Park, was discouraged with San Francisco. He had been called West, just seventeen years after the discovery of gold, to advise the ambitious young city about planning parks for its future, but he looked at the windswept sand dunes west of the built-up area and doubted that they would ever support so much as a single full-sized tree. Any parks, he felt, would have to be located in inner valleys and canyons sheltered from the wind.

The backbone of the park system he recommended was a man-made canyon along Van Ness Avenue twenty feet deep and as wide as a city block, terraced with shrubs and flowers; at the bottom, out of the wind, would be a broad landscaped promenade. But Olmsted was an easterner unacquainted with pioneer thinking. Men who had slogged across half a continent in Conestoga wagons and made fortunes in the Gold Rush or on the Comstock Lode were scarcely to be satisfied with a mere promenade and a few sheltered glades.

When the city received title to the western dunes all the way to the ocean in 1868, Mayor Frank McCoppin appointed a Committee on Outside Lands to make plans for the new area, including a large park. San Francisco, sand dunes and all, was not to be outdone by New York. In a day when parks were usually a few acres in size at the most, Olmsted's vast Central Park was spreading over 840 acres. San Francisco, still a mere village compared to New York, would obviously have to do better. The committee members blithely drew lines on a map extending from the geographic center of the city to the ocean—an area of a thousand acres. This, they decreed, would be known as Golden Gate Park. As a carriage entrance to the main part of the park, they planned a long avenue lined with trees and lawns (now known as the Panhandle). The committeemen were immortalized when the Panhandle cross streets were labeled with their own names in alphabetical impartiality: Ashbury, Clayton, Cole, Shrader, and Stanyan.

Olmsted was not the only skeptic. Critics said that the city had a white elephant on its hands, "a dreary waste of shifting sand hills," scoffed one editor, "where a blade of grass cannot be raised without four posts to support it and keep it from blowing away." The job of making a park out of this "dreary waste" was handed to a young civil engineer named William Hammond Hall. At the beginning Hall had no idea how the job was to be done; his principal asset was the kind of temperament that takes delight in tackling the impossible.

Looking over the terrain, he could see that the key to the park site was a three-hundred-foot hill, about halfway to the ocean, where some wild strawberries had found a foothold. West of Strawberry Hill toward the ocean was the windiest, sandiest area, and there he hoped he could grow some hardy varieties of trees, creating a wooded region. East of the hill, where there was a modicum of shelter and soil, he planned gardens and shrubs and began to set them out. It was heartbreaking work. Often the drifting sand buried his plantings and he had to start over. But gradually, over a period of years, at the extreme eastern end of the area, the sand began to give way to greenery, the dunes to lawns.

Olmsted, amazed at the results, wrote an enthusiastic letter to the young man who had proved him wrong: "I cannot too strongly express my admiration . . . There is no like enterprise anywhere else, which, so far as I can judge, has been conducted with equal foresight, ingenuity, and economy."

From the beginning Hall was plagued with politics. Everyone in the city, it seemed, considered himself a qualified park engineer. One faction felt that the park's design should be formal, that the entire site should be leveled off and made into something like the gardens of Versailles, with symmetrical

Golden Gate Park; meadow

plots of lawns, straight paths and avenues, fountains and statuary. Another group was opposed to the slightest tampering with the natural topography. Hall's method was to preserve the general forms of the land but to cut away occasional ridges for better access between valleys and to fill some of the arroyos for meadows and lawns—a plan that antagonized both factions. As a result Hall became the center of a political melee and after eight years as superintendent was forced out of office.

For a decade the park development continued under a succession of managers who followed Hall's basic design but who could not fill the shoes of the park's founder. Olmsted, by then the high priest of American landscape design, finally wrote the city a warning that a continual change of managements could lead to the park's "ruination." Hall had meanwhile joined the State Park Service, and when the furor over his policies died out had been appointed consulting engineer to the San Francisco Park Commission. He had his eye on a young Scotsman named John McLaren, who had been successfully developing large private estates down the Peninsula (and who had planted many of the long rows of eucalyptus that still line El Camino Real). On Hall's recommendation the young man was hired to carry out the herculean job he himself had only begun.

It was an inspired choice. For more than a half century John McLaren was the guiding genius of Golden Gate Park. The tales of his battles against sand, wind, politicians, and promoters have become legendary. Except for Hall's beginnings at the eastern end of the area, the drifting sand was still in control. To hold the drifts, McLaren sowed such hardy California natives as wild barley and lupine, but still the sand quickly buried them. He experimented with various grasses and finally found a European sea-bent grass that continued to grow as fast as the sand covered it up—eventually rising higher than the sand could reach. The first round was won.

Gradually over the decades the green oasis at the east end began to spread west. Fortunately for San Franciscans of generations to come the stubborn Scot would brook no interference with his plans from any source, and generations of officials who tilted with "Uncle John" retired licking their wounds. More than once he used his platoons of gardeners as an army to repel invasions. On one occasion when he found workmen from another city department removing trees and paving the area in front of the park police station, he mobilized his troops. As fast as the workmen poured in the cement the gardeners shoveled it out; McLaren won the day and replanted his trees. Once when promoters were given permission to build a trolley line through the park on the condition that their tracks would not disturb any vegetation, Uncle John and his troops quickly planted beds of flowers and groves of trees in the railroad's path. The baffled promoters withdrew.

McLaren was a good friend of a fellow Scot and kindred spirit, the great naturalist John Muir, and the two often hiked together on Muir's Sierra trails. Muir hated all cities, and on one hike—according to legend—he pointed to a waterfall plunging down a mountainside into a lake and taunted McLaren: "Do you have anything like that in the city?"

McLaren was undaunted. "No," he admitted, "but we will."

On returning to work McLaren stood appraising Golden Gate Park's only "mountain"—Strawberry Hill. Then he asked Park Commissioner W. W. Stow to put him in touch with somebody with money. Stow introduced him to the richest man in the city, Collis P. Huntington. McLaren took Huntington on a ride through the park and persuaded him that Strawberry Hill would be a fine site for a unique memorial bearing the Huntington name. The railroad tycoon was convinced and put up the funds. Today Huntington Falls cascades down Strawberry Hill into Stow Lake, and even John Muir had to admit that it was quite a sight—for a city.

McLaren was convinced that parks were for people. He refused to allow any "Keep off the Grass" signs and hated the statues that people were always donating to the park. He called them "stookies," and whenever one was set up, he promptly planted a wall of greenery around it. Years after his death, park gardeners were still digging the stookies out of the shrubbery.

Golden Gate Park; Stow Lake

Golden Gate Park; Panhandle

Inevitably someone presented the park with a life-sized stookie of Uncle John himself. His embarrassment was only temporary. He left the statue at park headquarters and never got around to setting it out. It was after his death in 1943 at the age of ninety-six that it was set out in a rhododendron dell especially designed by the park staff, who refrained from doing violence

Golden Gate Park; bridle path

to their boss's memory by putting the statue on a pedestal. Uncle John's feet are planted on the green earth he created from the dunes, and in his hand he holds a pine cone. Ironically, in order that the rare rhododendrons may be protected, McLaren Dell is the location of the park's only "Keep off the Grass" sign.

Golden Gate Park; bowling green

The efforts of Hall and McLaren to avoid formality and make the park as natural as possible have been given the ultimate seal of approval; wild animals by the thousands have adopted the park's woods and dells, its groves and meadows. Raccoons, squirrels, rabbits, skunks, foxes, possums, and weasels roam the park's more remote areas, and some species proliferate to the extent that one staff member is employed as a hunter to replace the natural predators and keep the wild-life population down.

Most of the species are not native to a dune area, and the park's greatest puzzle is how they got there across miles of built-up city blocks. One theory is that they come up the beach at night from the wild areas of the Peninsula, but no such migrations have ever been observed. Other migrations, however, are abundantly visible all over the park. In the spring and fall the lakes and ponds are way stations for great flocks of migrating ducks and other waterfowl; the only species in the park more abundant than the birds are the bird watchers, well equipped with binoculars and notebooks.

The most popular section of the park was created for a special purpose. M. H. de Young, the energetic publisher of the *Chronicle,* returned from the World's Columbian Exposition of 1893 in Chicago convinced that San Francisco should have an exposition of its own in Golden Gate Park. To many residents the idea was ridiculous; the country was by that time in the grip of a depression that had closed eighteen local banks. But de Young, in the same reckless spirit that caused Hall and McLaren to take on the sand dunes, insisted that the best defense was a good offense. Arguing that an exposition would stimulate business, he rallied the city's leaders, and the result was the Midwinter Fair of 1894–95. The fair was not only a surprising success financially; it made the park nationally famous and left some permanent assets—the sunken music concourse with its bandstand, the Japanese Tea Garden, and the de Young Museum, which was housed in the old exposition hall before the present permanent structure was built. The only reminders of the original hall are two stone sphinxes that once guarded its entrance walk, just east of the present museum.

The Tea Garden was the hit of the fair and continues to beguile visitors with its shrub-bordered paths and ponds, its moon bridge and miniature streams, its meticulously trimmed pine trees, its azaleas in the winter and its cherry blossoms in the spring. The garden has stimulated not only aesthetic admiration but international good will. On a small plot near the teahouse is a classical Japanese garden given to San Francisco by the people of Japan in 1952, and nearby is a big stone "Lantern of Peace," bought with contributions from the school children of Japan and "presented to the new generation of the United States as a symbol of friendship."

Golden Gate Park was not only the first park of its size to be created from sand dunes but ranks first in other respects as well. It possesses the first reinforced concrete bridge ever constructed in the United States—built

Ina Coolbrith Park

in 1889 on the main drive just northeast of Kezar Stadium—and the first major planetarium projector built in this country, completed in 1953 by the California Academy of Sciences. For more than a century the privately financed Academy has been a bulwark of the scientific community on the West Coast. It moved to the park, opposite the museum, after its downtown headquarters were destroyed in 1906. Besides the planetarium, its public activities include the operation of the Museum of Natural History and Steinhart Aquarium, both luring thousands of curious visitors every weekend, and the publication of *Pacific Discovery,* a distinguished magazine of natural science in the Pacific world.

Frederick Law Olmsted, in his original report, had recommended that San Francisco's parks should provide business people with opportunities for relaxation during the working day. Golden Gate Park is too far from the downtown area to satisfy this requirement, but the downtown workers who have the time and inclination for such profitable inactivity are apt to be found sunning themselves at lunchtime in Union Square or in tiny St. Mary's Square near the financial district. The latter park was established after the fire of 1906 to replace the unsavory nest of bagnios that once worried the Paulist Fathers of Old St. Mary's Church across the street and caused them to post under their tower clock a sign that still advises: "Son, Observe the Time and Fly from Evil."

Of all San Francisco's parks the richest in historical association is Portsmouth Plaza, the old town square where Lt. John Montgomery and his crew of the warship *Portsmouth* first hauled down the Mexican flag and raised the Stars and Stripes on July 9, 1846. Here Mormon elder Sam Brannan waved a whiskey bottle full of yellow dust from the American River and set off the Gold Rush. Here the Vigilantes administered frontier justice, and two decades later crowds gathered to watch the world's first cable car clatter up Clay Street under the proud eye of its inventor, Andrew Hallidie. The plaza is rich, too, in the variety of San Franciscans of many races and ages usually relaxing in the sun around the monument to Robert Louis Stevenson, who strolled these paths in the 1880's.

Fortunately, early-day city planners reserved a number of hilltops for

Portsmouth Plaza and old Hall of Justice

parks, providing tree-framed views of the city and bay. Pioneer Park on Telegraph Hill is the most popular of these green hilltops, but even more intriguing because of their quiet seclusion are such squares as Ina Coolbrith Park on Russian Hill, named for a California poet laureate, and the reservoir park not far away on Lombard containing a memorial to another poet, George Sterling, who composed odes to San Francisco ("O cool grey city of love . . ."). Other hilltop parks are Alta Plaza and Lafayette Park, both on

Pacific Heights. The former is an old rock quarry converted by the master hand of John McLaren; the sweeping stairs mounting its pyramidal terraces were copied from the grand stairway at the casino in Monte Carlo.

Lafayette Park is in some ways the Berkeley Square of San Francisco, as South Park was in a much earlier era. The big houses around the square are associated with great names of San Francisco's history—Spreckels, Phelan, Thieriot, de Young, Bransten, Scott, Henry Miller. Until 1936 the top of the hill itself—in the center of the park—was a privately owned plot occupied by a white mansion, a barn, and a windmill built by Samuel Holladay, owner of the Overland Stage Line. Holladay was a hard-shelled individualist who had lived on the spot since the Gold Rush and refused to move out when the park was created in 1867. Old-timers still know the area as Holladay's Hill. Next to the Holladay house was California's first observatory, built by George Davidson, the flowing-bearded pioneer scientist and savant for whom was named 938-foot Mount Davidson, the highest point in the city and the site of a 103-foot cross where Easter sunrise services are held. So successful was Davidson's Lafayette Park observatory that it led to the establishment of California's great mountaintop observatories on Mounts Hamilton, Wilson, and Palomar.

In 1901 President William McKinley and his wife stayed in the home of banker Henry T. Scott on the west side of the park, and because of Mrs. McKinley's illness the President held press conferences on the park's lawns. The great houses around the square were fortunately two blocks on the safe side of Van Ness Avenue, where the fire of 1906 was stopped, and immediately after the disaster the area became known as Bankers' Row. While refugees from the fire pitched tents in the park, the big houses flew the banners of the banks that had been burned out of their downtown quarters, and in their ornate rooms the bankers and business leaders planned the city's financial recovery.

In this city of vistas the most comprehensive panorama of all is seen from the treeless slopes of 922-foot Twin Peaks. The two summits are encircled near the top by an observation road; aside from a small reservoir and some utility buildings the road is the only "improvement" thus far on the city-owned property, which has long been scheduled for development as a park.

Palace of Fine Arts

Alta Plaza

The Spaniards called the peaks "Los Pechos de la Choca" in reference to a certain Indian maiden whose physical charms must have been abundantly evident.

Although the Presidio of San Francisco does not qualify as a park, the old military post contains large areas of green woods and fields, and in peacetime the army hospitably permits visitors in many areas, even providing picnic tables in a few locations. The Presidio, overlooking the Golden Gate, has remained an army post for nearly two centuries. The present Officers' Mess on the main parade ground is a reconstructed Spanish adobe that replaced an earlier structure there about 1791.

In a grove of willows, now the site of a picnic ground, is located one of the post's most remarkable but least-known features, a spring called El Polin, once legendary among the Indians. The aborigines believed that maidens who imbibed its waters during the full of the moon were guaranteed many children and eternal bliss. The local Spaniards, too, believed the waters to be miraculous, a conviction that would seem to have been confirmed in a very substantial way: General Vallejo had sixteen children, Argüello thirteen, Carrillo twelve, and Castro twenty-two. A number of the families using the water had several sets of twins each. Unfortunately the U. S. Army keeps no statistics in this matter on its own personnel.

After American forces assumed command of the post, they demolished El Castillo de San Joaquín, the crumbling old Spanish fortress on the south shore of the Golden Gate, leveled off the point, and built a handsome new brick fort, completed in 1860, along the lines of Fort Sumter. Its cannons were never called on to fire a hostile shot. Although it has long since been abandoned, Fort Point (the fort) still stands on Fort Point (the point). The building is also known as Old Fort Scott, as distinguished from nearby Fort Winfield Scott, thereby compounding the confusion.

The fort is now dwarfed by the Golden Gate Bridge; a huge steel arch especially designed to spare the historic landmark carried bridge traffic directly overhead.

Experts call the building one of the nation's finest examples of military architecture. Surrounding its main courtyard are several tiers of galleries, connected by ingenious spiral staircases and embellished with some of the

Fort Point

most artistic nineteenth-century cast-iron work in the United States. The air of mystery about the abandoned fort, with its weed-grown pavements, has occasionally attracted movie companies, which succeeded in shooting atmospheric scenes there despite misunderstandings with conscientious army sergeants who tried to be helpful by ordering their men to "police up" the old place for the picture in the best spit-and-polish tradition.

Some of the natural lakes that are now in city parks figured prominently in San Francisco's history. At the point where Park-Presidio Boulevard enters the Presidio from the south, just before it reaches the tunnel on the approach to the Golden Gate Bridge, is Mountain Lake, which was twice its present size before the road was built in 1939. This was the campsite of Juan Bautista de Anza, the steel-willed commander who in 1775 led an expedition of 240 men, women, and children 1600 miles from Mexico to establish a settlement at San Francisco the following year. He had left his charges at Monterey while he explored this area, and during the time his camp was at Mountain Lake he designated the site for the Presidio and the mission.

Flowing out of the lake is Lobos Creek, which enters the ocean at Bakers Beach and in the Spanish-Mexican era supplied water to sailing vessels anchoring offshore. Later it was the source of San Francisco's water supply. At the southwest end of the beach a red brick pumping station that now supplies water to the Presidio stands near the point from which the creek's water was once diverted to the city. A wooden flume built in 1858 carried the water along the shore line of the Presidio through a tunnel at Fort Point, another several miles along the bay shore and through another tunnel at Fort Mason to the foot of Van Ness Avenue. There a pumping plant lifted the water to the city's two original reservoirs on Russian Hill, both still in use. Along the Presidio cliffs, despite a century of wind, rain, landslides, decay, and wave attack, traces of the old wooden flume are still visible.

Several miles to the south of Mountain Lake, Laguna Puerca (also known as Pine Lake) adjoins Sigmund Stern Grove, San Francisco's outdoor concert hall. Oddly enough, although the spring-fed lake was remote from the built-up portions of the city until the 1920's, it was the site of one of the first

Presidio Cliffs; Bakers Beach; Sea Cliff

homes in San Francisco. In the 1840's a settler named George M. Greene built a ranch house there out of material hauled from his native Maine. After the Gold Rush, when the valuable lakeside property was coveted by other settlers, Greene built a fort and held off intruders until the legal title was secured in court.

Greene's son had several ideas for the improvement of the property. In the late 1870's he received his father's permission to plant the area with a strange variety of tree that had been imported from Australia; the trees flourished and became today's Stern Grove, one of the finest stands of eucalyptus in the state. In the 1890's young Greene decided that the area would be a good site for a resort, and he built the Trocadero Inn, which for decades was one of the city's most popular roadhouses. Political boss Abe Reuf used the Trocadero as his hideout after his machine was smashed in 1907, and he was eventually captured here by police. The old building still stands in the grove, little changed since its roadhouse days, even to the hand-painted washbowls.

George Greene, Jr., the son of the original settler, was still living in the Trocadero when he sold the property to Mrs. Sigmund Stern in 1931. Mrs. Stern had been convinced by John McLaren that a park on the property would make a fitting memorial to her husband. Summer concerts in city-owned Stern Grove often attract fifteen thousand people on a Sunday afternoon.

Southwest of Stern Grove is the city's largest lake—five-acre Laguna de la Merced. Near its southern shore is the campsite of the exploring expedition led by Captain Fernando Rivera y Moncada in 1774, and not far away a granite memorial marks the spot where Judge David Terry shot U. S. Senator David Broderick in 1859 in California's last and most famous duel.

Geologically the lake is even more significant. Once the area the lake now occupies was the mouth of a valley opening to the ocean. Probably during the same elevation of sea level that formed San Francisco Bay at the end of the last Ice Age, the valley mouth was invaded by the ocean and became an inlet. As the ocean current moved north, depositing great quantities of sand along Ocean Beach, it built a long spit that separated the inlet from the ocean. Streams entering the dammed-off inlet soon replaced the salt water with fresh. The overflow found its way to the ocean some distance to the

Ocean Beach

north before it was blocked off in the 1890's, when the lake was dammed artificially and its surface was raised for reservoir purposes. Although it is no longer maintained as a reservoir except as a stand-by supply, Lake Merced has found other uses; it was planted with trout in 1950 and has become the mecca of the city's fresh-water fishermen.

The same process of beach building that created Lake Merced goes on continually along the city's western boundary; among the most memorable sights in San Francisco is the view from the Cliff House along the great sweep of white strand to the south. Nowhere along this coast is there a finer display of breaking waves; the towering combers of a winter surf may break several hundred yards offshore and charge landward in a magnificent show of oceanic energy.

Most of the land surface on which San Francisco stands originated on this beach and was transported inland by the wind; the city was forced to find ways of curbing the sand drift lest the built-up areas themselves be buried. The answer was developed by John McLaren. To stop the drift he built a dam or dike along the beach, composed of timbers, cuttings from the park, and wire mesh. The drifting sand filled the spaces between, and the Great Highway was built on top. In strong gales off the ocean the sand still occasionally drifts over the road, and when the breakers pound with unusual ferocity they sometimes undercut it.

Less well known but even more spectacular than Ocean Beach is the area along the outer Golden Gate from the bridge to Point Lobos—a five-mile stretch of rocky beaches, small coves, and broken cliffs where the rolling waves continually batter the rocks and send up geysers of spray. It is perhaps here, strangely enough, along the rugged outer shore of the Gate, that some of the qualities that give this city its characteristic identity are most clearly visible.

Stand at Land's End and look out to the soaring span of the great bridge, to the ships passing through the channel, to the high cliffs on the far shore. A few thousand years ago this strait before you was the narrow channel of a river flowing to the sea—probably less than a mile wide at any point. Over the millenniums the assaults of the ocean have battered away these cliffs and flooded the river channel to create San Francisco Bay, broadening the strait to a width of several miles between the heads at Point Lobos and Point Bonita. Seal Rocks, Mile Rocks (where the lighthouse stands), and other scattered offshore formations are "sea stacks"—once part of the shore line but now surrounded and isolated by the advancing ocean. The advance is relatively rapid, and the area undergoes continual change. In some places along this shore of the Golden Gate the cliffs retreat visibly from year to year before the assaults of the waves. Here at San Francisco's doorstep you can observe the continual workings of the natural processes that created this city's incomparable setting.

The San Franciscan is perhaps better able than the residents of any other city on earth to sharpen his sense of values by continuous contact with the larger processes of nature and with immense perspectives of time and space. A city is more than buildings; it is more than people. It belongs to the particular part of the earth from which it has grown. The search for San Francisco's identity must be pursued not only among its steep urban hills, its crowded neighborhoods, its downtown commercial complex, but in the verdure of its parks, along its ocean boundary where the great Pacific combers roar, among the cliffs and coves of Land's End, where the continent and the sea meet in a wild and timeless encounter.

Seal Rocks

Telegraph Hill; east side

Muir Woods

Nob Hill; Taylor Street

The Poets' Follies

Pacific Heights; Broadway

Artists' Co-operative, Cow Hollow

Coffee Gallery

CHAPTER VII

The Arts

From the days of Edwin Booth to those of Jack London and William Saroyan, San Francisco has had a long tradition of bohemian colonies, but none has received as much publicity—for the wrong reasons—as the contemporary bohemia in North Beach at the foot of Telegraph Hill.

And few have been livelier. In the coffee shops and dimly lighted bistros along upper Grant Avenue, between the Chinese laundries and Italian ravioli factories, painters in sweatshirts display their canvases on the walls; amateur musicians launch impromptu jam sessions; youthful bearded philosophers expound the newest revolt, post their theses on the walls, and argue Ginsburg, Kerouac, and Zen Buddhism as solemnly as their predecessors once discussed Freud, Marx, James Joyce, and Picasso.

A surprising proportion of the Grant Avenue artistic activity has been successful in one way or another. Artists rent out old stores for galleries and sell paintings; jam sessions are often attended by capacity crowds; the City Lights bookshop sells thin paperbound volumes of verse by the local poets and records of some of the bards reading their own works. The poets find stimulation in presenting their works to audiences in regular readings and particularly in reciting poetry to jazz—for paying customers. Playwrights stage their own shows, also for paying audiences. The practical arts are well represented along upper Grant too, and the bars and art galleries are interspersed with the shops of artisans—leatherworkers, metalsmiths, photographers, weavers, and ceramists. Both craftsmen and artists display their works at one of the city's most lively festivals, the annual Grant

Upper Grant

Avenue Street Fair; poets, musicians, and dancers perform in the course of a day to crowds large enough to fill a football stadium.

By a series of accidents more related to the processes of modern publicity than to what was actually taking place there, the Grant Avenue bohemians in the late 1950's came to be known as members of the Beat Generation—"beatniks" for short. Some of the same people had congregated around the same area for years without attracting much attention, but when the new label took hold, reporters in search of colorful copy made forays into the sector—as if they were going into the Casbah—to write lurid "exposés" with such titles as "The Life and Loves of the Beatniks." The most colorful—or sordid—copy was of course supplied, not by the young intellectuals who were seriously interested in the arts, but by the semi-literate drifters and deviates found on the fringes of any bohemia. As a result, to most newspaper readers the term "beatnik" came to mean a kind of pseudo-intellectual delinquent with a beard, looking for kicks in marijuana, sex, cool jazz, and sadistic violence.

Among other bad effects of the beatnik stereotype was the fact that it obscured a phenomenon of genuine importance to an understanding of the city itself. What was happening along upper Grant could be understood, not in reference to the beatnik publicity, but only in a larger context of the character and traditions of San Francisco. The same phenomenon could not have happened in Kansas City or St. Louis or Detroit. It could be understood only as a part of a city where the arts have always been encouraged, where the artist—whether conventional or eccentric—could always find company, where art museums and symphony concerts have been known to draw more people annually than major-league baseball.

When the Giants, for example, announced their move from New York to San Francisco in 1957, press association headquarters in New York requested pictures of San Franciscans dancing in the streets. Of course there were no such pictures available. Although San Franciscans generally welcomed the Giants with enthusiasm, they were not thrown off balance by the event. It was not that they were too busy contemplating Van Gogh or Beethoven; by and large the city's residents have always been avid sport fans since the days when a gentlemanly San Francisco bank clerk named James J. Corbett was conquering the world of the prize ring. But San Franciscans have a sense of

Jam Session

proportion; they are also jazz fans, opera fans, and concertgoers. They are not too conservative to dance in the streets when they feel like it (on such occasions as New Year's—Oriental or Western style) nor is there anything unusual about taking the whole family to an art gallery for a Sunday outing.

One of the three big art museums, the M. H. de Young, ranks third in the nation in attendance and has more visitors in proportion to the city's size than any museum in the country; its annual attendance figure is about equal to the entire population of San Francisco. The record is due in part no doubt to the museum's convenient location in Golden Gate Park, but location is not the decisive factor. A Van Gogh exhibit in 1958 drew a quarter of a million paying visitors—nearly twice as many as the same show drew in the Los Angeles Museum in Exposition Park; a few years earlier an exhibition of Viennese art rang up more paid admissions than did the same exhibit in New York's august Metropolitan Museum in Central Park in the middle of a city nearly ten times the size of San Francisco. Appropriately in a city facing

Old Spaghetti Factory Café

the Pacific, the de Young prominently displays the arts of the Orient.

The other two big galleries are also well attended and distinctive. No museum in the world has a more spectacular location than the California Palace of the Legion of Honor, on a hill in Lincoln Park overlooking the Golden Gate. The third, the San Francisco Museum of Art, unlike the two other big, city-owned galleries, is privately maintained, though housed in the city's Veterans Building at the Civic Center. The museum holds frequent shows by local artists, emphasizes the contemporary in painting, design, and architecture, and sponsors programs of chamber music, poetry reading, and art films.

But the big museums are only part of the art scene in San Francisco. There are dozens of small galleries throughout the city, and on almost any Sunday scores of amateur and professional painters haul their easels and brushes to the city's squares and its heights, to Telegraph Hill or Golden Gate Park, or the Western Addition area of gingerbread houses. The

City Lights bookshop

M. H. de Young Memorial Museum

California School of Fine Arts on the northeast slope of Russian Hill gave birth to what European art magazines call the San Francisco School of painting, specializing in particular types of experimental abstractions. The city's Annual Arts Festival (the first of its kind in the nation) exhibits the work of thousands of artists and craftsmen in all mediums and on a single weekend draws more than a quarter of a million people who spend some $12,000 on art to take home.

Another indication of San Francisco's character as a cultural center is its emphasis on music. Eight thousand people, on the average, attend the concerts of the half-century-old San Francisco Symphony every week of the season. The popularity of the concerts requires the orchestra to hold three weekly performances rather than the conventional two. The San Francisco Opera Company, performing in the nation's first municipal opera house, is one of the three leading grand-opera companies in the United States. (The city also possesses the only permanent ballet company outside of New York.) And singers who may not make the opera—as well as some who do— still find noisily enthusiastic paying audiences in North Beach bars specializing in operatic music. Other night spots feature live chamber music. In that most American of all art forms, jazz, San Francisco is one of the three or four leading cities in the nation and has been the starting point for jazz musicians of stature from Paul Whiteman to Dave Brubeck.

The dramatic arts are popular here as well. There are four resident theater companies in the city, some of them often presenting productions of local playwrights—the Playhouse, the Interplayers, the Opera Ring, and the Actors' Workshop; the last was chosen by the State Department to perform at the Brussels World Fair in 1958.

It is significant that the San Francisco area is the site of two unique cultural institutions in the field of communications: KPFA (studios in Berkeley), the nation's first listener-supported radio station, and KQED, the number-one producer of programs for educational television stations throughout the United States. Both are supported by the community on a non-commercial basis and regularly broadcast programs of outstanding artistic and cultural merit.

There are other arts centers of all kinds, some across the bay, such as the University of California and the California College of Arts and Crafts in Oakland, some within the city, the latter ranging from the Poetry Center at San Francisco State College to the Cow Hollow area around Union and Fillmore streets featuring jazz and small galleries owned co-operatively by producing artists. The whole phenomenon has been analyzed in national magazines and even received the academic accolade when the University of California in 1959 established an extension course in the "San Francisco Renaissance."

This, then, is a city where the arts thrive. It is not necessarily a city that is producing great art in all fields, nor, as some enthusiasts assume, is it about to overshadow New York or Paris as an art center. But it has an atmosphere in which great art may yet emerge. The arts here are vital, creative, and popular. They are generally accepted as an important part of life in the city. It is at least arguable that per capita San Francisco devotes as high a proportion of its energy and attention to cultural matters as any other city on earth.

A vital part of any metropolitan center of culture is its bohemian colony, its Left Bank or Greenwich Village or North Beach, where young artists, poets,

Kid Ory

painters, and philosophers create a center of revolt against the prevailing standards of the society, a revolt expressed in dress and behavior as well as in paint and print. Inevitably the revolt inspires horror among the ultra-conservative and is damned as immoral by those who forget that a tradition of lively dissent—in the arts as well as in politics—is indispensable to a free society. Though most of the work produced in San Francisco's bohemia scarcely seems destined for immortality, upper Grant Avenue is nevertheless as essential a part of the cultural picture in San Francisco as the opera or the big museums.

To explain bohemia in terms of the city's cultural development, however, still does not account for the cultural development itself. What has made San Francisco a capital of the arts?

Part of the answer is that respect for the arts here is traditional. It can be traced back more than a century to the city's birth in the extraordinary sociological explosion of the Gold Rush. A frontier city is not normally considered a likely place for a development of the arts, but San Francisco was the exception. This city did not develop as an extension of an earlier frontier—as had most American cities—but came into being suddenly; it was a new society in a new land far from established centers of civilization. The discovery of gold, seeming to fulfill the ancient dream of a promised land in the West, attracted not only frontier stockmen and sodbusters but men of trained intellect from New York and London and Paris, as well as from Latin America and the Orient. It attracted students and intellectuals escaping Europe after the unsuccessful revolutions of 1848 and American college graduates who could see the opportunities of getting in on the ground floor of a society just beginning.

As a result of the extreme diversity of population in frontier San Francisco there took place the kind of cross-fertilization of ideas that always ensues when men of varied background come together in a new situation. The high educational level resulted in an emphasis on the intellect and schooling. By 1852 there were seven public schools in the city. Mills College, the University of California, and the University of San Francisco (or their predecessors) were all founded during the six years after the beginning of the Gold Rush.

The arts and sciences were well established during that period. Long before the first Vigilantes were formed to establish law and order, a traveling company of players was alternating circus performances with Shakespeare. In the same year there were some fifty printers in the community. Oil paintings adorned the walls of the best saloons. There were a dozen theaters and concert halls in the Gold Rush city and an even larger number of newspapers, including journals in a half-dozen languages. Just four years after the discovery of gold a group of San Francisco intellectuals founded the now-renowned California Academy of Sciences. The Mechanics Institute, which developed a fine library specializing in scientific subjects, was established two years later.

As the bonanzas of the Mother Lode were succeeded by those of the Comstock Lode and by even greater bonanzas in wheat, cattle, and

North Beach art gallery

Western Addition; Clay Street

eventually fruit and oil, San Francisco became the capital not only of an economic imperium but a cultural one as well. Men who made fortunes in gold and silver, in cattle and wheat and railroads, began to endow learning and the arts. The Mark Hopkins Art Institute, which later became the California School of Fine Arts, was one result. Leland Stanford established a university on his farm at Palo Alto and shook the academic world by presenting it with $20,000,000, the largest endowment ever made to a private educational institution.

Over the decades San Francisco produced or attracted numerous writers who later achieved fame—Bret Harte, Mark Twain, Ambrose Bierce, Joaquin Miller, John Muir, and in a later era Jack London, George Sterling, Frank Norris. Most important of all, the city developed an atmosphere in which the arts were encouraged—or at least not discouraged. The European influences and the lack of a Puritan tradition made the city relatively free of bigotry and censorship and produced an atmosphere of permissiveness favorable to the artist. In any era most of its bohemians have been young people who fled the confining restrictions of less tolerant cities to breathe the winds of freedom blowing through the Golden Gate.

A unique tradition, then, is one of the reasons San Francisco is a cultural capital. Another, equally important, is simply its natural location. San Francisco is a stimulating city partly because it would have been almost impossible to build a dull one in such a place. It has neither oppressive heat in the summer nor benumbing cold in winter. The cool salt breeze is a continual source of physical and mental vigor. The streets that seem suddenly to head for the sky or drop dizzily down from the hilltops, the presence of the waterfront with its ships from around the world, the continually astonishing views of hills and bay and mountains on the far shores, the delightful amalgam of inhabitants of every race and color—all these give the city a continual air of excitement, provoking the artist, the writer, the musician to think in new terms, to experiment with new forms, to soar off on new tangents of creative activity.

Because of an inevitable cultural lag this geographical impact—whatever its effect on subjective types of art—has not yet been fully felt in terms of an artistic expression of the city itself. Each new wave of "immigrants" brings its own attitudes from an earlier locale and an earlier tradition. Just as the architects of the San Francisco skyline for decades copied earlier styles before they learned gradually to break away from precedents, so the artists and writers often continue to paint and write in the older styles until the new environment can take full effect. Even those who are in conscious revolt are often more concerned with denouncing the old tradition than with the need for interpreting the new situation with new insight.

Yet there are beginnings of new forms and modes of expression in the Bay Area. The architects of domestic buildings have led the way toward indigenous expression of the city and the region; of all the fine arts theirs is forced to make the most immediate contact with the environment. The

Palace of Fine Arts

Earle C. Anthony Building

hilly building sites and the broad panoramas made conventional houses inappropriate and encouraged new concepts in housing.

The trail blazer in developing a regional style was Bernard Maybeck, a brilliant innovator who is ironically best known for his masterpiece in the classic tradition—the Palace of Fine Arts in the Marina. It was built as a temporary structure for the 1915 exposition but it was so hauntingly beautiful that despite its decaying condition San Franciscans could not bring themselves to tear it down, and in 1959 philanthropist Walter Johnson donated $2,000,000 toward its reconstruction in permanent form. Less well known is the fact that Maybeck was also the designer of the Earle C. Anthony Building, a startlingly ornate auto palace on Van Ness.

The architect's most famous work with indigenous forms is the Christian Science Church in Berkeley (completed in 1912), which for the first time imaginatively combined redwood with reinforced concrete and steel, leaving uncovered the natural textures of the materials. In San Francisco some of the same qualities, less fully developed, are found in the unique Swedenborgian Church on Lyon Street near the Presidio, built in 1895, a building for which young Maybeck helped draw the designs when he was working alongside another San Francisco innovator, Willis Polk, in the office of Arthur Page Brown, designer of the Ferry Building.

Maybeck's houses—such as the Leon Roos residence at Jackson and Locust, and the Goslinsky house on Pacific near the Presidio—similarly broke away from convention. A key to understanding his work is the special use by modern architects of the words "honest" and "natural," referring to the lack of artificial adornment and the undisguised use of the materials. Whether Maybeck used redwood or concrete or steel, he did not try to hide the material or pretend that it was something else but ingeniously made the most of its own inherent possibilities. He pioneered, for example, in the development of the beamed ceiling, and instead of cutting off the ends of rafters as if they were something to be ashamed of, extended them and carved them to develop their own aesthetic potentialities. Abandoning the conventional idea that a house must be rectangular or box-shaped, he developed "open planning," spreading out the floor plan to add more windows, light, and air and to vary the relative positions of the rooms. He loved greenery and in the design of his "natural" houses used outdoor shrubs and trees as a part of the architecture. He did not limit himself to large houses but carried some of the same principles into the field of low-cost dwellings. Probably his most remarkable house was his own residence in Berkeley constructed of potato sacks dipped in concrete.

Like Willis Polk, Maybeck was decades ahead of his time, but unlike Polk, who died in 1924, he lived to see the times catch up with him. He died in 1957 at the age of ninety-five, after a new generation of architects had paid him the supreme homage. They had rediscovered his innovations and carried them further, using materials naturally (particularly redwood), enlarging the windows, and opening the house plan even further to develop the possibilites of indoor-outdoor living. Their work has been hailed in the United States and Europe as "Bay Region Style." There are numerous exponents of this approach (most of them insist it is not a "style") but the best known are probably Gardner Dailey and William Wilson Wurster, the latter dean of architecture at the University of California.

Although architecture has led the way, there are beginnings of regional expressions in the other arts as well. With the passing of time the painters and photographers become more aware of the Bay Area's unique qualities of light and landscape. The jazz musicians experiment with styles expressing

the moods of the city, from the exuberance of the traditional Dixieland to the sophistication of modern cool jazz. San Francisco's close ties with the Orient are reflected in Japanese influences in home decoration and in paintings of California landscapes that resemble those of Japan, with its luminous hills and drifting fogs. The sculptors experiment with works composed partly of natural objects—native wood, pieces of stone, shells from Pacific beaches.

Even in the work of the local fiction writers and poets, who often seem concerned only with introspection or with a purely negative rejection of conventional standards, there is occasionally visible a response to the stimulating qualities of this landscape, a glimpse of its potentialities. Highly perceptive expressions of various aspects of the city are found in the best work of such writers as Jack Kerouac and—at the opposite pole—Herb Caen.

But perhaps this land is still too new for full expression in literature or most of the other arts. With few exceptions it has not yet been seen with fresh vision stripped of preconceptions and of reactions to older environments. There has been no Thomas Wolfe to walk the streets of this city by night; no Walt Whitman or Carl Sandburg to explore it by day, grasp its tone and significance, celebrate its beauty and harshness and vitality.

The city awaits its artists, its composers, its poets. Someday a painter thinking in new ways will suddenly see the Golden Gate Bridge as if for the first time and capture its meaning in potent line and color. Someday a poet, walking on a beach or exploring an alley or climbing a hill, will be seized by a vision of this place, and he will set down his vision on paper, and for the first time there will be words that begin to express the essence and identity of this city at the continent's end.

California Palace of the Legion of Honor

U. S. 101 near Golden Gate Bridge

East of Twin Peaks

Parkmerced

From Bernal Heights

Pacific Heights

South of Twin Peaks

Edgehill Heights, near Mount Davidson

Embarcadero; Pier 15

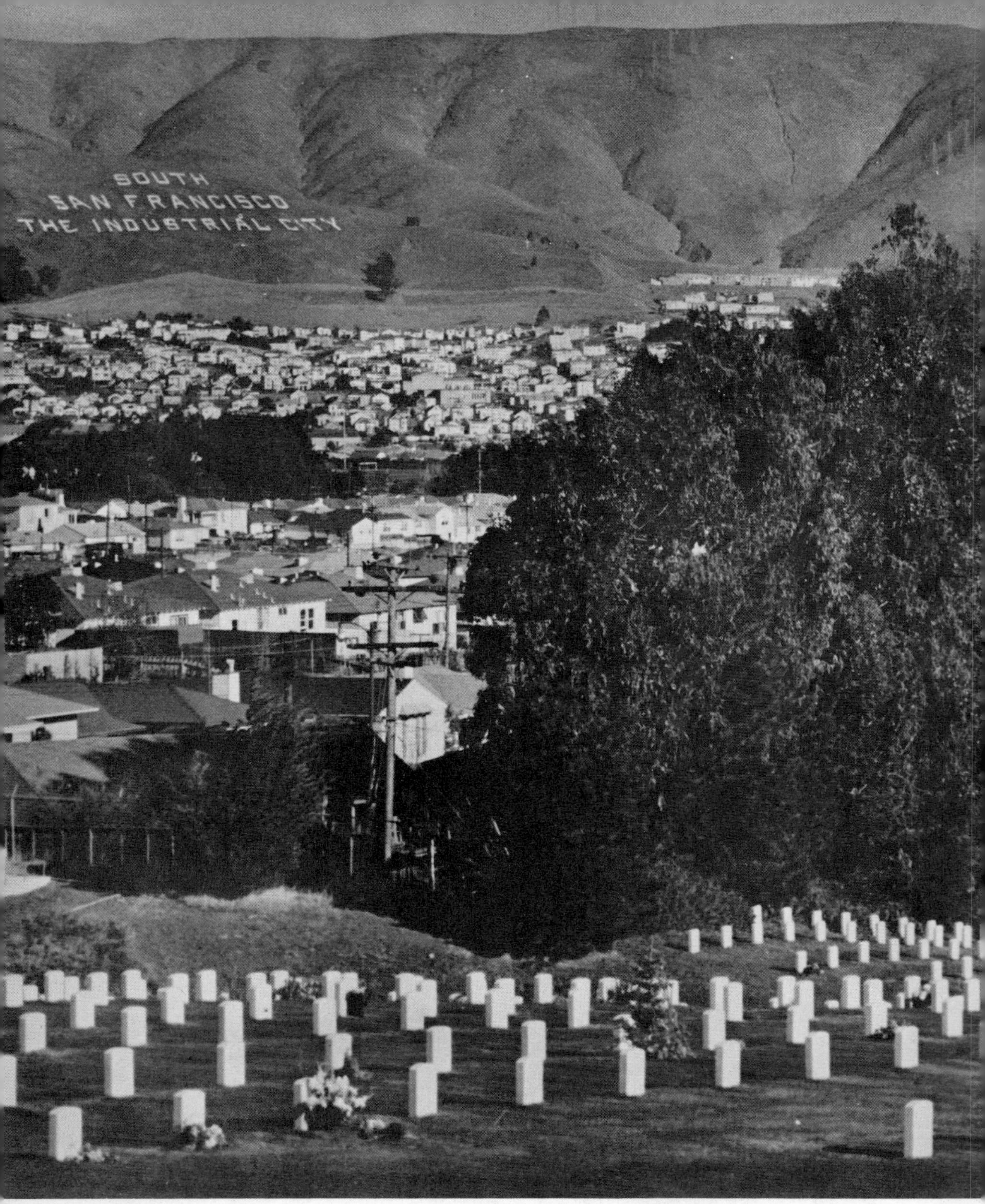
SOUTH
SAN FRANCISCO
THE INDUSTRIAL CITY

Golden Gate National Cemetery, San Bruno

Hyde Street

The Burnham Plan; Telegraph Hill

CHAPTER VIII

The City of the Future

Just as mountain ranges, in the long stretches of geologic time, are scarcely more permanent than waves on the surface of the ocean, so too the face of a city, as buildings rise and fall in the shorter periods of human history, is temporary and evanescent.

Many aspects of today's San Francisco would be scarcely recognizable to anyone who had last seen the city several decades ago, and it seems certain that the next few decades will bring even greater changes. No one can accurately predict the appearance of the future San Francisco, but one thing can be said with assurance: the kind of a city it is to become will depend on the degree to which its growth is planned or chaotic.

Generations of visitors have been deeply impressed with the potentialities of the city's location. Four decades after the Gold Rush, James Bryce, British author of *The American Commonwealth,* found San Francisco the most exciting city on the continent in terms of natural setting: "Few cities in the world can vie with San Francisco either in beauty or the natural advantages of her situation; indeed, there are only two places in Europe—Constantinople and Gibraltar—that combine an equally perfect landscape with what may be called an equally imperial position."

Sixty years later another European, the architect Eric Mendelsohn, expressed the same feelings, but with some reservations: "There is no town, no city in the world—ancient or new—that could compete with the potential 'city beautiful' of San Francisco. I say potential because we have too often neglected its very assets and possibilities."

Like Mendelsohn, San Francisco's most discerning citizens have often recognized that in some respects their city is beautiful not so much because of what man has done as in spite of it. Shortly after the turn of the century a group of community leaders brought to San Francisco the nation's foremost city planner, Daniel H. Burnham, and his assistant, Edward H. Bennett, and charged them with developing a plan for "the improvement and adornment of San Francisco" comparable to Burnham's designs for Chicago and Washington, D.C. Burnham moved into a house built for him by Willis Polk on the slopes of Twin Peaks, a location still marked by present-day Burnham Street. From there he looked down on the city and rebuilt it on his drawing board.

When he presented the plan, San Franciscans were deeply impressed by its sweep and grandeur. Like most planners of the time, Burnham had been fascinated by the rebuilding of Paris by Baron Haussmann for Napoleon III a few decades earlier, and the Burnham Plan for San Francisco was essentially Paris with hills. From the Civic Center at Market and Van Ness, broad boulevards radiated out in all directions intersecting another series of boulevards circling the city, with a kind of a Place de la Concorde at each main intersection. Park-lined streets followed the contours of the hills. From Golden Gate Park the Panhandle was to be extended to the Civic Center as a long mall. Burnham envisioned Twin Peaks terraced in a grand classic style resembling the gardens of Versailles. The city's water supply would arrive at the highest point of the peaks in a colonnaded triumphal entrance, cascading down the slopes to lakes in the midst of formal parks and groves.

Burnham had scarcely presented his plan when, as if by design, most of the city was leveled by the disaster of 1906, clearing the ground and presenting San Franciscans with a matchless opportunity to build a planned city. But the frontier spirit was still too strong; the individualistic San Franciscans had not had time to become accustomed to the concept of city planning. They were understandably in a hurry to erect shelter for the homeless and places where business could be resumed, and the city rose from the ashes without benefit of planning. Burnham's plan died an untimely death, and San Franciscans were in no mood even to consider large-scale planning for at least another half century.

Perhaps in some ways it was just as well. Burnham's plan, though

North from Twin Peaks

commendable in sweep and boldness, was essentially an adaptation of European ideas, and had it been followed, San Francisco today would be a quite different city. Compare, for example, Burnham's plan for Telegraph Hill, including large classic apartment buildings and solemnly formal gardens, with the spontaneity of the present-day hill, where modern apartments, middle-aged houses, prefire cottages, and rambling gardens are delightfully jumbled together all over the steep slopes. It is this same kind of verve and variety that gives the entire city much of its individuality. The surprising, the eccentric, and the unexpected, however sharply they may clash with formal aesthetic standards, result in a city far more vigorous and colorful than one laid out according to the rationally regulated uniformity of the total planners. It is impossible to imagine a lively bohemia, for example, developing among the well-ordered gardens of Burnham's Telegraph Hill.

Yet Burnham's plan is well worth consideration, not for its details, most of which have been outmoded, but for the boldness of its approach and for the light it throws on future planning. As San Francisco enters the final four decades of the twentieth century, this city of paradox is confronted by the most profound paradox of all: In the past the city's uniqueness, its individuality, its incomparable variety and diversity developed spontaneously, with very little planning of any kind: in the future it is probable that these qualities can be maintained only by planning—and planning on a scale far greater than any now officially under consideration.

The reason is geographical. In the 1950's the city completed a century of horizontal growth. With the subdivision of the last sand dunes in the city's far southwest corner, the limit of horizontal expansion was reached. But even the most conservative estimates indicated that the population of the Bay Area would more than double in three decades. It was increasingly being said at the end of the decade of the 1950's that an expanding San Francisco had no place to go but up. The statement was most frequently made to back up arguments for taking off the lid, for an absence of all restrictions on future building. Yet without planning, what can be expected to happen to San Francisco is what naturally happens wherever population pressure builds up in a geographically limited area.

As property on the tip of this narrow peninsula becomes more scarce in relation to population and hence more valuable, skyscraper business buildings will rise higher and crowd closer together, and skyscraper apartments will mushroom from the hills in increasing numbers until the city is a dense jungle of mass dwellings and commercial buildings, each blocking the other's light and view. San Francisco will become a West Coast counterpart of Manhattan Island, its diversity and individuality submerged in a gray uniformity of concrete and asphalt. At the core of this unlimited vertical development will be the kind of sordid slum areas that degrade human life in all cities that have failed to plan for the future. The low-income groups, unable to afford the expensive skyscraper apartments, will increasingly crowd together in blighted blocks of decaying buildings in the older, lower areas of the city.

If this is the kind of city San Franciscans want, all they need do is let nature take its course. The alternative to such a chaotic development is to plan future expansion in such a way as to retain and emphasize the city's unique character.

The main physical factors that have traditionally given the city its uniqueness are its flavorsome old buildings, its waterfront, its lack of large-scale slums, its hills, its parks, its climate. All of them, even the equable climate, will be drastically impaired or eliminated by unplanned growth. All of them can be preserved and enhanced by planning.

Planning need not necessarily be official. Some of the best examples of planning to enhance these values have been set by private individuals and groups. Perhaps the best example downtown is Maiden Lane, which was once simply an alley off Union Square lined by the backsides of retail stores. Co-operative planning by the merchants and imaginative designing converted the lane's two blocks into one of the city's most distinctive shopping areas. City officials agreed to prohibit vehicular traffic during the middle of the day, and the lane has become a popular noon-hour promenade. Its most noted shop is the V. C. Morris store, the only building in the city by Frank Lloyd Wright and the only retail store ever designed by him.

Another example of private planning is in the old Barbary Coast quarter, where dilapidated but picturesque old buildings were ingeniously rehabilitated by private developers, trees were planted along the streets, and the

Maiden Lane

Jackson Square

area—renamed Jackson Square—became the city's wholesale decorative center. A key unit in the Jackson Square development is the iron-shuttered Hotaling Building, a one-time distillery headquarters, which survived the fire of 1906 and was thereupon immortalized by poet Charley Field:

> *If, as they say, God spanked the town*
> *For being over-friskey—*
> *Why did he burn the churches down*
> *And spare Hotaling's whiskey?*

Not far from Jackson Square, a Victorian office building at the triangular corner of Columbus and Kearny was similarly transformed by redecoration into one of the most attractive structures in the city, full of good humor and refreshing eccentricity. Now called the Columbus Tower, this building, too, survived the fire, and one might have similar reasons for wondering why. It was built around the turn of the century by the very symbol of corruption, "Boss" Reuf, and it was from his office on the top floor that he ran the city for several years, before he was transferred to a less elegant address—San Quentin.

Action to rehabilitate the city's old buildings has also been taken in such residential areas as the block south of Alta Plaza and the Green Street block on Russian Hill just west of Leavenworth, where old Victorian houses have been handsomely redecorated. The Telegraph Hill Dwellers Association, a neighborhood improvement group, encouraged the sprucing up of old buildings on the hill, and the hill's property owners themselves have refurbished century-old houses in such a way that they are far more attractive than many of the neighboring glassy modern apartments. All of these citizen groups and private owners were motivated by the realization that their city's character did not lie in its qualities of chrome and glass and neon but in its unconventional diversity, its preservation of the best qualities of older eras, its love of originality and eccentricity.

Citizen action on a far larger scale was responsible for the development of grandiose plans for the Golden Gateway Project, a combined commercial, apartment-house, and park development sparked by the downtown business-

Columbus Tower

men of the Blyth-Zellerbach Committee to replace the blighted produce district and provide the city with an impressive eastern entrance. The project was basically a demonstration of the kind of citizen initiative and leadership badly needed to develop the city on a planned basis.

Similarly bold plans have been made for the Embarcadero. The San Francisco Port Authority, a state-supervised agency, plans to remove most of the docks north of the Ferry Building and relocate them in the industrial area south of Market, where there will be more space for dockside storage of cargoes. An "Embarcadero City" would rise in their place—office buildings, hotels, shopping centers, yacht facilities, restaurants, and a large auditorium.

It is to be hoped that this plan for remaking the waterfront, admirable though it is in many respects, does not end in eliminating the waterfront. The planners should not lose sight of the fact that one of the city's most unique qualities is its intimate relation with the sea and the ships. Perhaps in no other city in the world is the drama of the freighters and ocean liners entering the docks, loading and unloading their cargoes from around the world, so clearly visible and immediate as along the northern Embarcadero, particularly as viewed from Telegraph Hill. Every effort should be made to retain in this area as much shipping activity as is economically feasible and to develop even further this great scenic asset by providing, both in the old dock area and the new, views of the dockside activities and the ships— from roof-top restaurants and observation points overlooking the piers and the bay.

At another level of planning, spontaneous action by residents was responsible for forcing highway engineers to reconsider the network of freeways they had planned to stretch across the city bisecting residential areas. If the special character of San Francisco is not to be obliterated by the "tyranny of the automobile," if increasingly larger areas of the city are not to be devoured by freeways, parking lots, vast garages, and floods of cars, other means must be found to transport masses of people in and out of town. One answer may be in the Bay Area Rapid Transit District's plan for a network of subsurface high-speed rail lines linking the city with other bay communities.

Embarcadero (present)

Embarcadero City (planned);
Golden Gateway Project at bottom

Western Addition

Although San Francisco has so far lacked large-scale slums of the kind found in older cities, it is well on the way to developing them, particularly in the Western Addition. Landlords have found it profitable to divide and redivide the crumbling Victorian houses to accommodate more tenants. Speculators with more shrewdness than conscience purchase blocks of the old buildings and resell them to the city at jacked-up prices for redevelopment purposes. Although the city's long-delayed slum clearance and redevelopment program began to make headway by 1960 with the clearing of large areas in the Western Addition, it had yet to solve a major problem: The old houses held low-income tenants, but the new buildings to be put up in their place by private developers are designed for high-income groups; low-income housing is seldom profitable. The evicted tenants often must move into other old buildings nearby, thus aggravating the overcrowding problem and creating more slums. If private developers cannot do the job, the only way to break this vicious circle would seem to be more government-built housing for a wider range of low- and middle-income groups. Otherwise the slums seem destined to spread like an infection to ever-widening areas of the city.

Nothing contributes more to San Francisco's character than its hills.

Although no one has yet planned to level them off, their identity would be destroyed by an unrestricted Manhattan-like growth of skyscrapers. An ordinance which became effective in 1960 gave the City Planning Commission greater power to create height limits in residential areas by restrictive zoning. Although the restrictions were considered by planners to be the maximum politically obtainable, they were nevertheless far from adequate to maintain the present character of the hills.

A grim lesson in what can happen with unrestricted development is plainly visible on Russian Hill. In the 1920's a ten-story apartment house was constructed on Green Street, on the eastern brow of the hill, with large view windows on the east side overlooking the city and bay. A few years later the owners of the adjacent property built a thirteen-story apartment house, leaving residents of the first building a fine view of a blank wall—a couple of inches away. The 1960 ordinance could not prevent the same thing from happening to existing buildings. What is needed is legal recognition that property rights, in hilly San Francisco, include "view rights." The hills should be developed primarily for the benefit of the people who continue to live there rather than the profit of the speculators.

Nob Hill

It is of course neither possible nor desirable to halt the processes of change that are transforming the face of the city, but it is possible to make and enforce zoning restrictions in such a way as to preserve the essential character of such unique areas as the upper slopes of Telegraph and Russian Hills. The greenery of the hills, their diversity of dwellings, their alleys and steps and winding pathways affording continual pleasant surprises for the explorer by foot, their panoramas of the city and the bay—all will rapidly disappear behind oppressive walls of concrete unless there is bold and diligent planning.

Despite its limited area San Francisco has always seemed a spacious city —a fact attributable not only to its hills, which give the residents views extending far beyond their own immediate neighborhood, but to its parks and squares—particularly the green wonderland of Golden Gate Park, which exist only because of the vision of its early leaders. To maintain the city's spaciousness, that vision will have to be matched by the present generation in providing additional parks as the population increases. In recent decades provisions for new parks have lagged far behind the city's growth, and a sunny Sunday afternoon at any time of the year finds most of the parks and squares jammed far beyond their reasonable capacity.

Near Marina Yacht Harbor

In terms of park space per resident San Francisco ranks behind most other large Western cities. If every resident of the city were to seek park space at the same time, there would be about 240 people crowded into every acre of every park in the city—as opposed to an equivalent figure of 232 people per park acre in Oakland, 218 in Los Angeles, 174 in San Diego, 71 in Pasadena and 68 in Portland. (San Francisco's park figure is sometimes distorted by counting the 1480-acre Presidio as one of the city's parks, even though large parts of the Presidio are closed to the public and much of the rest is occupied by military installations.)

Not only has there been in recent years little effort to acquire more parks, but existing parks and potential park areas are continually threatened by pressure from those who look upon any green space only as a potential sub-division. At various times responsible officials have proposed to sell part or all of several existing parks in order to "put more property on the tax rolls." And it is the perennial ambition of would-be subdividers to acquire most of the Presidio and convert its potential park areas into housing tracts. San Francisco is already one of the five most densely populated cities in the United States, and there is no doubt that the even more crowded city of the future will need all the breathing space obtainable.

In view of the lack of any effective large-scale planning at an official level in San Francisco, it is one of the city's more extraordinary paradoxes that its planning department has been cited as one of the finest in the nation. The department has developed a master plan for the city, including rejuvenation of the downtown area with trees, small parks, and subways; expansion of neighborhood parks; enlargement of the Civic Center; redevelopment of blighted neighborhoods—all designed to preserve and enhance the city's characteristic individuality. The plan might be criticized for being too timid, too conservative in its estimate of how much planning is politically feasible; but, minimal though it is, the master plan has been consistently ignored.

City officials have not hesitated to ignore or override the planning depart-ment in many areas—for example, in its recommendations to require new skyscrapers to be constructed in such a way as to permit light and air into the streets; its recommendations to prevent tall, view-blocking apartments in such areas as Russian Hill; its recommendations that land released by the federal government be acquired for parks. Sometimes San Francisco's incomparable natural advantages seem to be matched only by its determination to destroy them.

Almost without exception these breaches of sound planning have been committed in the name of economy. It must be admitted that San Francisco, because of its geographic limitation, has special financial difficulties. About one quarter of the people who use San Francisco's facilities—its streets, parks, terminals, museums, police, public buildings—pay no direct taxes to support them. They are commuters and others who regularly come into the city for business or pleasure. San Francisco's residents must pay extra taxes to make up the difference. At the same time influential downtown property owners who do not live in the city pay a large share of the property taxes. As a result, from both residents and absentee owners there is continual pressure on public officials to get more property on the tax rolls. Parks pay no taxes; subdivisions and large buildings do. The formula is simple: to collect more taxes, add more subdivisions and more skyscrapers—without limitation. In the long run, of course, this formula defeats itself by jamming more people into an overcrowded area and creating a need to spend more money to cope with the resulting congestion.

Meantime, the qualities that make San Francisco a unique place to live in and visit are gradually being eroded away. With even a small measure of the vision and initiative that made San Francisco "the city that knows how," ways could be found to raise money without blighting the city in the process. Numerous solutions have been suggested: a commuter tax, a parking tax, a tax on incomes earned in the city, and a Bay Area tax in which San Francisco would share. Many authorities believe that the growth of the entire region demands an over-all Bay Area agency to administer at least such common facilities as harbors, airports, bridges, regional parks, and rapid transit and to deal with such common problems as smog and pollution of the bay. The form the agency should take is debatable, but the logic of the general principle seems inescapable. Some such agency should develop a regional master plan to cope with a doubled or trebled population, with special provisions to acquire immediately the land that will be needed for parks and open space.

What is required is a recognition that San Francisco and its neighboring cities have outgrown the boundaries drawn a century ago. The Bay Area has become a single community. It includes the spreading residential and industrial complex of the East Bay, with the metropolitan areas of Richmond, Berkeley, Oakland, and Alameda, the regional parks and campuses. It includes the Peninsula, with burgeoning subdivisions on the east and redwood forests and beaches on the west—areas that can provide much-needed breathing space for the future if they are acquired as parks and not all lost to commercial development. It includes rapidly growing Marin County to the north, which can have some of the nation's finest park areas along with its mushrooming subdivisions—if action is taken in time to prevent such destruction as occurred in 1959, when a large grove of virgin redwoods on Mount Tamalpais was logged over by lumbermen after it had been

Marin County; Drake's Bay

designated for acquisition as a state park. (Lumbermen similarly destroyed large portions of the forest on Marin's Point Reyes Peninsula after that region was recommended for inclusion in the national park system.)

And, finally, the Bay Area community includes the bay itself, a superb natural asset that has given the region its greatest value as a place to live. Like many other of the area's natural advantages, the bay is diminishing under the pressure of population. The eagerness of many communities to fill in the bay to add more property to the tax rolls can only be self-defeating. The destruction of large areas of the bay will affect the climate; by diminishing the circulation of air, it will intensify the already-serious smog problem. It will make necessary incalculable future expenditures to combat flooding of

Bay and city from Belvedere Lagoon

filled areas resulting from the long-term rise in sea level. It will destroy not only present commercial and sport fishing but the enormous potential of the bay—once the pollution is cleared up—as one of the world's richest fisheries. It will eliminate the possibility of using the bay—as contemplated in the Reber Plan—for conservation of the great quantities of fresh water that flow into it from the Sacramento and San Joaquin rivers and are wasted out the Golden Gate. It will destroy the educational and scientific benefits of the animal life inhabiting the bay and its shores. And it will destroy aesthetic and recreational values that can never be measured on a balance sheet. Obviously an over-all Bay Area agency should have the power to restrict filling of the bay in the interests of long-term conservation.

On all counts the lesson is clear: The qualities that give San Francisco and the Bay Area their unique advantages will continue to disappear without long-range planning, both by communities and by the region. Without planning, the San Franciscan of the future, if he is able to find a vantage point not blocked by skyscrapers or clouded by smog, will look out across a filled-in bay and intolerably congested areas of asphalt and concrete inhabited by millions of harried urbanites who know little of the values of green grass and blue water or the calmness of occasional solitude in woods and fields or an uncrowded park.

With vision and planning, the San Franciscan of generations to come will still live in a city that would be recognizable to its present-day inhabitants. He will walk on downtown streets made pleasant by trees and flowers, some of them closed to automobiles entirely. He will ride subway trains conveying him at high speeds from downtown to any part of the Bay Area. He will have the opportunity to find refreshment and renewal, to sail in the bay on a weekend, hike through the woods on Mount Tamalpais, explore the unspoiled beaches of Marin and the Peninsula. He will cherish in actuality—and not merely in memory—the San Francisco of hillside cottages and gardens, green parks, cellar cafés, cable cars, and eccentric old buildings, a city where great expanses of water or hills are always in view and on summer afternoons the smell of clean salt air and fog drifts up the steep streets from the bay.

Marin County; Richardson Bay from Belvedere

Richardson Bay Bridge; Mount Tamalpais

(OVER) *Angel Island*

U. S. 101, Mill Valley

Aquatic Park turntable

Index

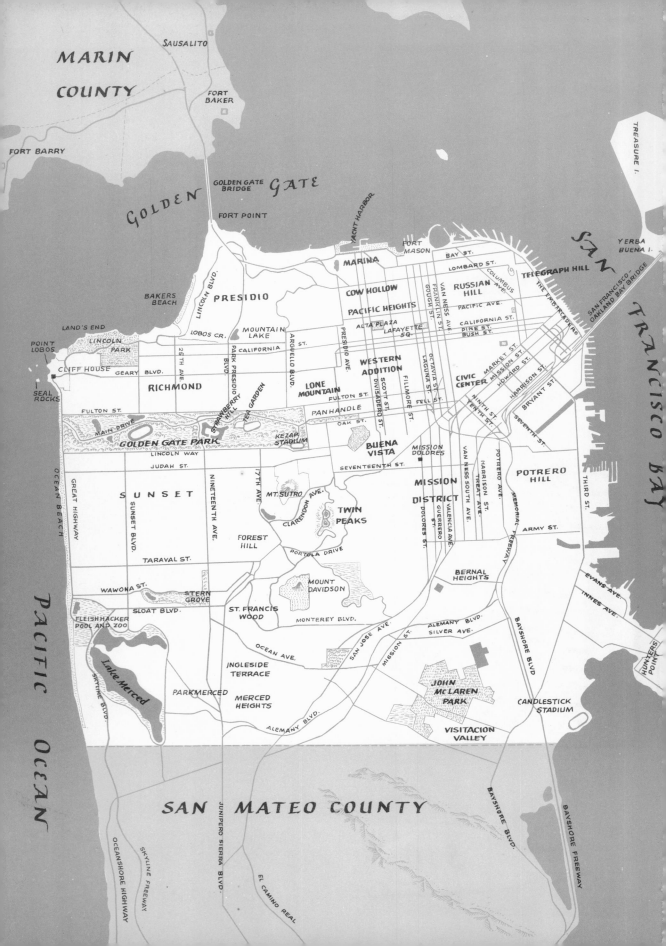